SO YOU WANT TO START A SUBSCRIPTION BOX

THE DEFINITIVE GUIDE TO LAUNCHING AND GROWING A PROFITABLE SUBSCRIPTION BOX

LAUREN PRENTICE

authors
AND CO.

CONTENTS

INTRODUCTION

So you want to start a subscription box? But you don't know where to start? You know that the industry is booming and that the time to start is now, but there are so many moving parts to figure out: suppliers, billing cycles, the tech…

In 2020 I was in the same position as you. I knew that I wanted to start a subscription box, I knew that my box would be a hit, but getting all the different bits and pieces lined up to launch my box seemed like an impossible task. I launched not one but two boxes that year and have since grown them into two multi-six-figure businesses.

Perhaps you've got a great idea for a subscription box, or you know that this is the business model you want to start your new business in. You might even have more than one awesome idea, you're just not sure which one to run with. But you're stunted because you don't know where to turn next, you don't know which avenue to go down and information sources out there on starting a subscription box are few and far between.

The truth is, it's not hard to have a six-figure subscription box. It's easy when you know how. As subscription boxes are based on a recurring revenue model, a box costing £30 per month needs fewer than three hundred subscribers to hit a £100,000 turnover in a year. I believe that achieving this milestone is possible for everyone, no matter what their background, box idea or previous business experience.

In 2020 when the pandemic hit, I was running several successful businesses. Within days, all four of my businesses were mothballed. Not only were they unable to operate, but because my main business was within the theatre industry, I was faced with having to refund hundreds of thousands of pounds. As the lockdowns in the UK went on and on, I knew that I needed to pivot in a major way. I looked at industries which were growing and – more importantly – were pandemic proof. Subscription boxes popped up time and time again as the best option for me. Since then, I have launched two subscription boxes and bought another. Within twelve months of launching my boxes, I reached the one thousand subscribers mark.

When I began, my boxes were completely bootstrapped, with no funding and no spare cash to burn. I am going to teach you how you can do the same, how you can have a six-figure subscription box without needing lots of money to get started.

For so long, recurring revenue has seemed like the unicorn of the business world. Everyone wants it but so few manage to achieve it. With a subscription box, you'll be able to add a recurring revenue stream to your business, meaning a predictable income, constant cash flow and reassurance that you won't be chasing invoice payments.

I have had countless clients go from box zero to box hero by following the same blueprint that I outline in this book. I've had clients who have launched their box and had three hundred subscribers within the first week alone, and others that have been able to significantly change the way that their business previously operated due to the amount of recurring revenue their subscription box now makes, allowing them more time freedom to spend on the things that matter.

Throughout this book, I will show you the steps you need to take to have a successful, profitable subscription box. I'll teach you how to grow your audience, research and find out exactly what your ideal client wants from your box, have a successful pre-launch so that you don't need lots of start-up cash to make your box a success, and how to reduce cancellations so that your box is constantly growing. I am going to show you how to launch, grow and scale a profitable subscription box business.

So, without further ado, let's begin your subscription box journey so that you can become a wealthy subscription box entrepreneur.

1

WHY A SUBSCRIPTION BOX?

If you're reading this book you're probably already converted to the subscription box is the business model for me' camp. However, I want to reassure you that you've made the right choice. The subscription box industry is booming. It's an industry that in many parts of the world is still in its infancy. Even in the USA, where subscription boxes have been part of life for some time, there is still a lot of growth to be had and ample opportunity to take your share of the market.

Subscription boxes are a relatively new phenomenon. However, that doesn't mean that they're not in demand. The excitement and consumer demand for convenience, joy and discovery through subscription boxes have never been higher.

Gone are the days of people worrying about subscribing to something and having to commit for any length of time.

Today's consumers are primed and ready to commit to subscriptions.

Royal Mail (in the UK) predicted in 2017 that the subscription box market would grow by 72% by 2022. However, that growth has been far surpassed with the help of the pandemic and the fact that people's buying habits have changed substantially post lockdown.

Royal Mail repeated their survey in 2021 and found that 45% of Londoners were signed up to a subscription box. They also predict that the market will be worth £1.8 billion by 2025; there is no better time to start a subscription box.

When it comes to subscription boxes, the phrase 'the riches are in the niches' has never been more prevalent. If we look at the USA where the subscription box market is more mature than in other countries, we can see that they have subscription boxes in every niche going. There are hugely popular tinned fish subscriptions, balloon modelling subscription boxes, boxes for Christian women, a tea towel subscription box and a whole host of other weird and wonderful boxes. This is without mentioning the more generic mainstream boxes which are less niche but no less popular, like Dollar Shave Club, Hello Fresh, Smart Ass and Sass and Glossy Box.

By looking at our friends in America it is easy to see the scope and scale of the subscription box industry and to see how this will be replicated in other countries in a few years.

Being the 'founding father' of your box within your industry and being the first in your niche to launch a subscription box will not only make you the original box which others will aspire to be like but will also mean that you're the first to offer this kind of service to your ideal customers, without much in the way of competition and not within a saturated market. This is a very rare opportunity to enter an industry in its infancy, to start something without lots of competition and before the industry booms.

Passive income or recurring revenue has often been thought of as the 'unicorn' of the small business world. And although subscription boxes are not passive income, I am going to teach you in this book how to make your subscription box as passive as possible and how to automate the steps along the way so that you have a consistent, sustainable recurring revenue stream.

DIFFERENT TYPES OF SUBSCRIPTION BOXES:

I have a strong belief that there is a subscription box in everyone. So often I'll be speaking to someone about subscription boxes (one of my favourite topics) and they'll say, "I'd love to start a subscription box of...". There is a subscription box in everyone.

However, that's not to say that the market is over-saturated or that someone else will already have thought of your idea. Plot spoiler – there are plenty of people to go around and even if there is a similar box out there to yours, there are plenty of opportunities for your box to shine.

There are subscription boxes for everything, particularly in the US. Other areas of the world where the market is still in its infancy have fewer choices, but that doesn't mean that the opportunity to make money from a subscription box is any less. One of my favourite pastimes is checking out the various boxes for sale on Cratejoy.com, a marketplace platform a little like Etsy or Amazon but specifically for subscription boxes. There is a whole host of weird and wonderful subscription boxes on there. Anything from a box for Christian women to a box about wrestling, a box of tinned fish to a box to learn how to balloon model, a box of cheese to a box of bones for the archaeologist in the family!

The sheer wealth of different subscription boxes out there simply proves that there will be a market for your box, no matter how niche it might be. The more niche your box is, the more likely it is to be a hit, but more on that later.

There are two main types of subscription boxes, which most, if not all boxes fall into.

THE REPLENISHMENT BOX:

A replenishment box is a box which tops up / keeps you supplied with (usually) a household item. This could be a subscription box containing dishwasher tablets, toilet rolls, cat litter, toothbrushes, or another household item that you have to buy regularly. A replenishment box means that subscribers have one less thing to think about; they know that their essentials will be delivered without them needing to think about it, or without having to dash out and grab them when they're down to their last few items.

Replenishment boxes are growing in popularity. They help busy customers automate their household items and give subscription box entrepreneurs the chance to capitalise on people's need for convenience. It also means that people can get their hands on brands and items that they wouldn't be able to get in the supermarkets as easily and readily as a subscription. For example, the Smol washing tablet and dishwasher tablet subscription means that subscribers get an eco-friendly alternative to chemical-filled supermarket versions, in recyclable packaging and at a cost saving too, without having to dig for an eco-friendly version in the supermarket. This model is being replicated time and time again and you can have anything from your toilet paper to your cat litter to your dog food as a regular delivery.

Amazon has added their subscribe and save option which has proved popular for several years to enable people to subscribe to receive their favourite items frequently. If that's not a testament to our growing demand to have our household items delivered without us needing to do anything, then I don't know what is.

By nature, replenishment boxes tend to have a lower churn than discovery boxes. This is because people rely on the convenience of receiving these items regularly and don't want to have to go back to remembering to purchase them when they need a top-up.

DISCOVERY BOXES:

Most boxes fall into the discovery box category. They're sending a box of items to the customer which is a surprise or a pre-chosen selection of items. It's helping the subscriber to discover new items and new brands as well as delivering them an experience when they come to open their box each time it lands on their doormat.

Discovery boxes give your subscribers a great opportunity to have a fantastic experience. They have the joy of receiving something that is within a niche that they love but they also get the element of an expected surprise. Just like a baby loves the expected surprise of 'peekaboo' we love to receive delivery of surprise items that we know have been curated especially for us.

That doesn't mean that discovery boxes are only boxes of fun items like beauty boxes or book boxes, they can also be more practical. For example, my box The Business Box is a discovery box, but it also has the dual purpose of helping subscribers build their business. On the flip side, some would argue that Hello Fresh is a hybrid of the two box types. Although the items inside it are very practical (all of the ingredients to make a meal) which suggests that it is a replenishment box, the fact that subscribers are allowed to sample new recipes and flavours in each box makes it a discovery box. This is probably partially a reason for its success as they manage to combine the two models so successfully.

A HYBRID OF THE TWO:

There are some boxes which are a hybrid of the two different models. They're a little bit of replenishment and a little bit of discovery too. For example, a wax melt box would fall into both categories: subscribers are being replenished with wax melts each month but are also getting to experience different scents that they wouldn't necessarily pick themselves. Generally, a hybrid box will always tend to be a box of consumable items in which flavours, scents or colours are switched out each box to add the fun, discovery element.

DIFFERENT TYPES OF SUBSCRIPTIONS AND MEMBERSHIPS:

Subscriptions are a normal way of life for us in the twenty-first century, even if we don't realise it. Sure, there are the obvious ones like a dishwasher tablet monthly delivery and a magazine subscription, but I bet that if you were to look at your household outgoings, you'd have at least ten recurring monthly payments outside of your essentials like gas, electricity and water. Subscriptions are part of our daily lives and there's no reason why you can't have a piece of the recurring revenue pie.

Take the obvious ones, for example. You've got your TV subscription (ok, you might not have anything flashy) but most of us have a bolt-on with our broadband for TV too. Maybe you add sports or kids' channels. Yes, that's a subscription. Whilst we're on the subject of TV, what about Netflix? There are thirteen million Netflix subscribers in the UK. I bet that wouldn't be something you'd be willing to give up easily even if you're not binging series every evening.

What about food? We've all got to eat, but do you have any memberships or subscriptions within your food bill? Perhaps you subscribe to a food box like Hello Fresh or Gousto, or maybe you have a delivery pass for a supermarket? If big businesses like Tesco and Asda are getting in on the recurring revenue business model, when they are traditionally bricks and mortar businesses, then there are ways for every business to introduce recurring income.

Tesco has even gone one step further and has introduced a scheme by which, for a set amount, you can save 20% on four shops each month. Sounds fairly straightforward, doesn't it? But there's a lot more to it and it's a genius scheme. Firstly, the money off only applies if you shop in-store when you physically do the shopping yourself. We all know that when we go to the supermarket we get sucked in by offers and bargains and Tesco know that too, which is why they want to encourage you into the store where you'll buy clothes, books and electricals amongst all of the other things they offer these days. Not only are Tesco getting your monthly membership fee, but they're also getting your loyal customers. It's a genius subscription.

What about your other shopping habits? Aside from the boring food shop how else have businesses introduced recurring revenue? There are very few people I know who aren't subscribed to Amazon Prime. Amazon has managed to find a way to fulfil our need for instant gratification and to dominate the market for not just books and tech but anything else we could need.

On the flip side, what about Costco: perhaps you have a Costco membership? Costco is a magical place. You enter and instantly feel like you cannot leave without 'making use of your membership' or in other words, leaving with a trolley full of bulk buy items. Costco has a particularly interesting membership model. Firstly, their membership is somewhat exclusive (or at least that's what they advertise). You can only sign up if you run a business or if you work in a certain selection of sectors. In truth, most job roles legitimately fall into one of those sectors. But the fact that it seems exclusive makes people want to sign up. Costco is particularly interesting to me as they make the large majority of their money through their membership fees. They don't have a huge markup on their products and although they do make a profit on them, their main source of income is from the membership fees that their customers pay each year.

How about your kids? (If you've got them?) Maybe you take them to classes like football, cookery, baby sensory, or who knows what other weird and wonderful educational opportunities are on offer in this weird and wonderful world we live in. The activity provider will have you sign up for a monthly or termly package of sessions; they'll most likely ask for the money upfront. You guessed it, another recurring revenue.

It even applies to our furry friends. What about your pets? Even village vets can get in on the recurring income carnival with schemes for monthly worming tablets or flea treatment or puppy or kitten schemes to see them through their first years with spaying and vaccinations. These schemes guarantee that as a pet owner, you'll be returning to that same vet time and time again and if anything does go wrong with your pet (and we all know how pricey that can be) that we return to that same vet that we've built a relationship with.

And that's not even to mention the added subscriptions that we as business owners subscribe to. Perhaps you're in a membership to help grow your business? Or maybe you've got a monthly payment going out for your email provider, web hosting, or insurance? The list is endless.

This doesn't even scratch the surface of things that we see as a luxury. Perhaps you subscribe to receive a subscription box each month. There is plenty of awesome subscription boxes out there including my own The Business Box. I truly believe that there is a subscription box in every business and that the subscription box industry, which is already worth $122.7 billion in the USA, is about to boom not just in the UK but the rest of the world. Now is the time to get into the subscription box space, when it's ripe for the picking and you can become the market leader in your box genre.

If you take a look at Cratejoy, the leading platform for subscription boxes in America, you can see more weird and wonderful subscription boxes than you could ever imagine. Boxes for fly fishing enthusiasts, Christians, Montessori nursery activities, clay pot making, tie dye crafting, wrestling fans, tinned fish and all number of things you'd never think were either necessary or popular.

Although these subscription boxes are often seen as a luxury, there are plenty which helps the time poor with the essentials. Take Dollar Shave Club, for example, which sold in 2016 for $1 billion. Their simple business model of sending a monthly delivery of razor blades and shaving foam/balm etc. helped them to grow a ridiculously successful recurring revenue business with a rumoured four million subscribers.

And they're not the only ones. There are subscription boxes out there for vitamins, herbs and spices, pet food, toothbrushes and all the other essentials that we buy on a day-to-day basis.

In short, the whole household is covered with revenue replay opportunities, which is why it's so crucial that you find a way to include recurring revenue in your business. There is no better way to do this than by starting your own subscription box business. With the market booming around the world and consumer demand for different boxes growing day in, and day out, there is no better time than now.

A recurring revenue stream from your subscription box business will be a game changer for you. Knowing that you have a consistent, predictable revenue stream not only brings security but also means you will have the regular cash flow to invest in your business.

Research &
Development

2

RESEARCH AND DEVELOPMENT

IDEAL CLIENT:

Knowing your ideal client is key to the success of your subscription box. Not only will it help you to build something that your audience actually wants and needs, it'll help you to really get a grip on your messaging and will make your launch process much simpler. When you're creating content and writing emails and posts with your ideal client in mind, you'll be talking directly to them.

When we talk about an ideal client avatar, it's a fancy way of saying 'the perfect customer'. The ideal client is someone who, if all of the stars aligned, would drop on your doorstep begging for your box. Although this seems like an impossible dream and something which would never happen in real life, once you've established who that client is and have adapted your messaging to suit them, you'll be halfway to that becoming a reality.

You should know your ideal client as well as you know yourself. In fact, if you are following your own passion (and we all know that profit follows passion) your ideal client will often be remarkably similar to yourself.

The things that you need to know about your ideal client are far-reaching: you should know their age, occupation, how many children they have, who they live with, where they live, whether they own their own house, their income, their pets, where they shop, their ethics, their values, whom they vote for and everything else in between.

I must point out that I'm not suggesting this is a real person. I'm not for a minute suggesting that you track down one of your clients and find out their bra size, medical history and what they ate for breakfast this morning. That would likely result in you being served a restraining order and that's not the aim here.

Your ideal client avatar is a fictional character whom you have created. They may not exist in real life. (In fact, it's highly unlikely that you'll ever find one client who has the exact traits, likes and dislikes as your fictional character.) However, your 'real life' ideal clients will have many similar traits, likes or dislikes and will relate to the messaging you're putting out into the world because of this.

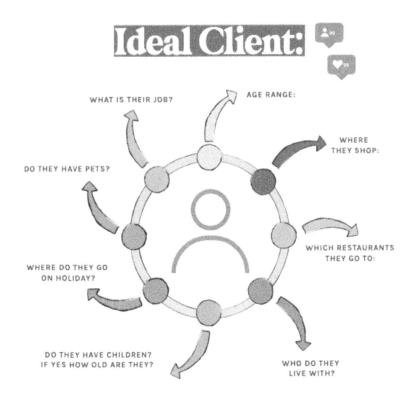

THEIR PAIN POINTS:

One of the most important things for you to recognise when it comes to your ideal customer is identifying their pain points. These don't have to be hugely profound. They may be things that keep them lying awake at night worrying or they may be things that they want to improve in their lives. Knowing all of these details will help you to work out what will serve your ideal customer best. How can your box solve these pain points? By tailoring not just your messaging but your whole offering to solving these pain points you will have a recurring revenue stream that people will be crying out for and will remain subscribed to long into the future.

If your box can solve any of the big pain points below, then you're on to a winner.

What keeps your ideal client up at night? What do they worry about? Who do they worry about? Do they have financial worries? Are they stressed on a daily basis? If so, what about?

However, solving the smaller pain points is just as valuable.

Like, what do they feel guilty about? What do they dread doing? What do they love doing but don't have the time for?

My Nutritional Ninjas Bake Box is for busy parents who want their children to have less screen time and want to enjoy more quality time with them. However, as they are busy working parents time is at a premium and they need to have stress-free activities to do with their children which require little or no tidying up. Our bake box solves this problem by pre-measuring all the ingredients for each bake, meaning there's no weighing, no big bags of flour for little hands to clap together causing a flour bomb, and no rushing to the shops for last-minute ingredients while the child sulks because they want to bake *now!* By removing these stress factors like the cleaning up and supply of all the ingredients, as well as removing the need to decide which recipe to make, we solve this major pain point for our ideal clients and ensure that they can simply enjoy quality time with their children, with minimal stress.

Doing ideal client work involves digging deep and can sometimes bring up quashed feelings from the past, especially if your ideal client is very similar to you. However, rest assured that by doing this work, you'll be helping yourself to help more people with your subscription box and in turn have a growing and flourishing business.

Knowing your ideal client's pain points is key to delivering something that they are not just going to want but are going to need too. You want to create a subscription box which is not just a luxury but something which they feel that they need and cannot live without, that they will see as an essential. The best way to do this is to solve the pain points that your subscribers need solving.

I really can't stress enough how important knowing (and solving) your ideal client's pain points are. Although it seems inconsequential and a little bit gimmicky, knowing the information about your ideal client inside out is not a stage in the process that you can skip and still expect great financial results from your subscription box. My coaching clients who know their ideal client inside out are the ones that see the quickest and biggest results: don't skip this step; regard it as step one on your journey to success.

HOW TO IDENTIFY YOUR IDEAL CLIENT:

Figuring out who your ideal client is should be a fun activity. This is the ultimate game of make-believe through character building. In the same way that an actor builds a back story for their latest character, you are building your character to take on the role of your ideal client. Imagine that you're creating a character for a story, only the story is your business. You need to ask a few fundamental questions. However, these are only the basics. The deeper you go with these questions, the more and more you'll be able to tailor what you offer to the people that you actually want to be serving and in turn will be tweaking your messaging to appeal to them.

The basics include:

What gender are they?

How old are they?

Where do they live?

Do they have children?

Where do they shop?

What do they worry about?

What makes them happy?

What are their aspirations?

These answers form the basics of your ideal client. Next you need to use this above information to create a bigger, clearer picture of who your ideal client is. See the graphic below for an example of this. Use the graphic to build a strong ideal client avatar.

Insert graphic: (spider diagram of different questions linking off of this)

I know my ideal client for The Business Box inside out. I know that she is a female between thirty and forty-five who lives in a property that she owns, has run her own business for more than one year but fewer than ten years, that she enjoys social time and quality things. I also know that her pain points include not feeling supported within her business, not having anyone to celebrate her wins with, worrying that she won't hit her business goals and that she's also often lonely working as a solopreneur.

By knowing all of these details, I know how to position not just all of my messaging but also my pricing and the products that go into The Business Box each month so that they suit my ideal client and bring her joy. The box itself is something she looks forward to each month, but, because we offer monthly trainings and hot seat calls, I know which experts will be best to bring in to support my ideal client, and ultimately all of these elements help me to reduce my overall churn and help me to retain customers.

And remember, your ideal client doesn't have to be set in stone. Things can change as your business develops and grows. You can add things as you get to know your fictional ideal client better and discover new things, which will help you to better serve your existing and potential subscribers.

WHAT ELSE ARE THEY SPENDING THEIR MONEY ON?

It's really important to consider what other things your ideal client is being tempted to spend their money on. What other things are competing for your ideal client's money? If your box is a luxury box or not considered an essential then it is really important to consider what other businesses are competing for their ££s. This could be any number of things. For example, if your box is a children's craft box, you should consider other children's activity boxes from your competitors, but it's also important to think outside of the box (if you'll pardon the pun). Your competition for their money could also be craft classes, products in craft stores, craft kits sold in supermarkets as well as a whole host of other things vying for their money.

It is important to be aware of the things that they may also be spending money on and to be aware of the prices that they may be paying for these things. However, if these items or services cost less money, this doesn't mean that that they won't be looking to pay for your box. It does mean, however, that you'll need to really nail the messaging as to why your box is ideal, for example, reminding people of the conve-nience, excitement and value of your box being delivered to them will help potential subscribers to forget about the other things that are also vying for their cash.

CUSTOMER VERSUS CONSUMER:

The difference between the customer and the consumer is hugely important to note and something that can't be ignored. The customer is the person who is buying your box. In many cases, they are both the customer and the consumer if they're buying the box for themselves. However, in many cases, the customer (the person buying the box) and the consumer (the person using and enjoying the box) are different. This is the case for my Nutritional Ninjas Bake Box: the box is bought by the parent or the grandparents and consumed by the child (the consumer). This is the same for any box designed for children or younger teenagers, boxes for pets or even for subscription boxes which are designed to be gifted such as a box for new mums.

For many of us, we've got double the work to do as our customer and consumer are different. We need to know our consumer and our customer equally as well. Knowing this information and targeting your messaging and advertising appropriately can be a gamechanger. This is the case for Poo-pouri, the toilet spray to remove poo odours. Their messaging is driven towards women, who are buying the product to reduce the stench left by their partners after going to the toilet.' They market to women with cheeky fun content and solve the problem that their ideal client suffers with – that of bad odours from their partners (the consumer).

YOUR IDEAL CLIENT AND FACEBOOK/ INSTAGRAM ADS:

It's important to mention as a side note how important it is to know your ideal client if you ever decide to run Facebook or Instagram ad campaigns to grow your subscription box.

Facebook ads can be a magic bullet for twenty-first century business owners. Gone are the days of companies paying big bucks to have their TV commercial shown during an ad break in the hope that their ideal client might be watching. Now we can tailor our adverts to be served to exactly the right people, those that really and truly are your ideal client.

You can stipulate exactly who you want to target and narrow down through age, location, family demographic, where they shop, who they support, what their ethics are. It's a magical tool and great for rapid growth of any subscription box. I'll be talking about this later in the book but by having all your ideal client research done early on in the process of setting up your subscription box, it'll help you further down the line when it comes to running paid ads.

RESEARCH:

If you're like me, you've probably got multiple, multiple ideas for different subscription boxes and that's no bad thing!

However, when you've got lots of ideas it's super important that you have your finger on the pulse as to which idea is the most viable, which is going to be in demand with your ideal client and also which is going to be the most profitable. After all, you could have the most fantastic idea, but if your ideal client doesn't want that type of box, then it'll be tricky to get it off the ground and will cost you lots of time and money in trying.

Research is crucial for any business, but it's even more crucial when you're starting a subscription box business as you're asking people to commit to spend with you each month. The more research you do, the better position you'll be in in the long run when it comes to launching your box. You'll not only know your ideal customer and your target market's needs, wants and desires inside out but you'll be in the strongest position possible to have a thriving, profitable subscription box.

CUSTOMER RESEARCH:

In the ideal client chapter, you read how important it is to research your fictional ideal client and to know them inside out. However, when it comes to customer research it is all about the importance of finding out more about the 'real' ideal clients and using that research to make your box perfect for them.

The best way to do this initial customer research is through an online survey that you post anywhere your ideal customer hangs out. The simplest way to do this is to build a Google form and to ask your ideal customers a range of questions.

When putting together your survey, be sure to not overwhelm those taking it with too many questions; ideally, they should be able to complete it in two or three minutes. There are a couple of questions you'll need to include to make sure that the people completing your survey are your ideal client. These could be questions about gender, age or whether someone has children; the questions will of course differ depending on the type of box you're making.

You need to include a few key multiple-choice questions to help you to make the decisions around your box. These could be based around the frequency of delivery, the price that people would be willing to pay for the box or the number of items they'd like to see in the box. For these questions, the answers you're looking for are based on quantity. You're looking for how people answer each question in percentage terms, so you can see how the answers are spread across the participants to work out the consensus.

When it comes to asking open questions, it is wise to keep these to a minimum to ensure that your survey is simple to complete and that the information you garner is useful to you. I find that asking people who they follow in terms of influencers and social media pages is a valuable question as it gives you a shortlist of the people that they're keeping up with and could also give you some names should you choose to later do an influencer campaign.

I strongly recommend incentivising people to complete your survey, for example, by offering them a prize draw entry for a free box or a small prize. However, make sure that the prize is relevant and specific to your ideal client. You don't want lots of people who aren't your ideal client completing your survey simply to try and win and thus skewing your results.

One thing to remember is that sometimes you need to take the answers with a 'pinch of salt'. People may say that they want eight items in a box for only £10. It goes without saying that this isn't necessarily practical, and I would argue that it probably means those people are not necessarily your ideal clients and haven't really considered the practicalities of a subscription box and how it works.

Using your survey can be a fantastic way to start building your audience. I always suggest including a box where people can enter their email address to be entered into a competition. (Make sure that the competition prize is only relevant to your ideal client so that you don't get lots of people entering who aren't your ideal client simply to win a generic prize.) When you have people's email addresses (ensure that they're properly opted in to comply with GDPR) you can start to email them on a regular basis to keep them up to date on the progress of your box and its impending launch.

Once you have your survey results make sure that you sit down and analyse them properly. Take a look at the answers, both those that can be quantified and the answers to the open-ended questions to ensure that you are tailoring your box to the ideal client you're catering for.

FOCUS GROUPS:

As you get closer to launching, running a focus group of a handful of your ideal clients will be really helpful in giving you the confidence to know that you're on the right path for your box.

A focus group can be in person, or it can be online over a video call. Hosting a focus group closer to when you launch is most valuable as it means that you'll be able to ask questions and gain feedback on the elements of your box that you're now near enough set on. This can be about the items you'll be putting in the box, the number of items in the box, prices, and also finding out how they will be attracted to any offers or promotions that you have planned.

COMPETITOR RESEARCH:

When starting your box or even when well established, it's key that you always have an eye on what your competitors are doing. That's not to say that you should be copying what they do or worrying about what they're doing and allowing imposter syndrome to slip in, but it is super important that you've always got one eye on what they're doing so that your box can evolve, be better and bring your subscribers a more exemplary experience.

KNOWING WHO YOUR COMPETITORS ARE:

This seems like an obvious task. Obviously, your competitors are other boxes within your niche. For example, my children's bake box The Nutritional Ninjas Bake Box has lots of competitors; there are plenty of other children's bake boxes out there so parents have plenty of choice. However, that's not to say that they're our only competitors. When a parent is looking for a subscription box for their child there is a whole world of different boxes for them to choose from. Let's assume that they are looking for a box which encompasses an activity. That means that they're not just looking at baking boxes but also craft boxes, gardening boxes, STEM boxes and all the other activity boxes out there to choose from. For this reason, as a children's activity box it is super important that we have a finger on the pulse of not just all the other baking boxes out there but the other activity boxes that parents will be presented with when it comes to searching for a box for their child.

On the other hand, with The Business Box, we know that at the moment we're the only 'real' box within the UK within our niche. (There may be others, but they're generally smaller and not well known or established and although we keep an eye on these, they're not really considered competitors.) However, as our primary market is female business owners and self-employed women, we need to keep an eye on the other resources available to them that may also compete for their money. For example, memberships, short courses, and masterclasses. This is because if a business owner has set aside a certain amount of money for self-development each month within their budget, it's likely that they'll make a choice between The Business Box and one of these competitor products.

LOOK INTERNATIONALLY:

Whether you intend to ship your box outside of your home country or not, it's worthwhile checking out boxes similar to yours in other countries. One of my favourite places to do this is on Cratejoy.com which is a marketplace for all sorts of different subscription boxes. Have a look for what these boxes are offering that you're not, but also look at what you're offering that they're not. This way you can get a clear picture of the strengths and weaknesses of your own box.

REVIEWS:

When looking into your competitors, look at their own social proof, whether that's reviews, articles or social media posts. Have a look at the various reviews and really dig deep to think about what people are saying. If all of the reviews are five stars, it suggests that something fishy is going on and that perhaps the box owner has been filtering out the lower graded reviews. Also, when it comes to one-star reviews, this is usually something to be wary of too. Very few people who want to give genuine feedback will give a one-star review. They'll tend to give a more measured response, so one-star reviews are often from people who have been vexed in some way. Of course, this may be for genuine reasons, but often these are reviews to be wary of. The reviews with the most 'clout' for your research purposes are the three-star reviews. These will give you the most insight into things that people like and dislike about the box and the service that they've received. Always take any reviews with a 'pinch of salt'. As much as you can garner lots of information from them, remember that for someone to make a review they need to invest time and energy into logging into whatever platform is being used and actually writing a review, so someone needs to feel quite strongly about their opinion to do so.

LOOK AT WHAT GOES IN THE BOX:

It seems obvious but it's important to evaluate what goes in the box. See if your competitors include any items which are similar to items you're planning to put in your own box. Can you spot which suppliers they've come from? Evaluate the quality of the items: are they the same, lower, or higher quality that you'll be offering in your own boxes? Does the box have a luxury feel? Or is it more basic? Also check how many items they're putting into their boxes. Some will have lots of items which all cost less whereas others will have fewer items but with higher price points or a higher quality.

When you're looking at what your competitors have put in their boxes think about it with your ideal client in mind. For example, the biggest competitor for my Nutritional Ninjas

Bake Box is a company that does baking kits for kids, but they don't include any refined sugar. Their box is fantastic and hugely popular; however, we don't share the same ideal client. Our ideal client isn't so worried about organic ingredients or coconut sugar versus regular sugar. What they want is convenience. The fact that all of our ingredients are pre-packaged and that they only need to supply regular store cupboard ingredients is a massive hit for our subscribers. In conclusion, while from the outset it might seem like we have the same ideal client, when you dig down deeper, we have a very different ideal client and as such, there's plenty of room in the market for both of us.

WHERE THEY ARE ADVERTISING:

One of the things that will reveal the most from your research is looking at where your competitors are advertising. Are they running paid ads on social media, are they using Google AdWords, are they doing lots of PR, are they listed on lots of marketplace style websites? You can dig through and see where they're advertising manually, and this is a very good task to do, but you can also use websites such as semrush.com. When you enter your competitor's website address, they'll reveal which sources their traffic is coming from. Be warned that there is a charge for this, but to avoid this you can do the legwork yourself and see where your competitors appear to be getting their traffic from.

ANALYSE THEIR SOCIAL MEDIA:

The next step in your competitor analysis is to look at their social media. What are they posting? Stories, images, infographics, pictures, reels? But most importantly what kind of content is being engaged with the most by their followers? Is the content that they put out conversational or educational? Is it mainly targeted at signing subscribers up or are they adding value?

Also have a look at their tagged images. Are their subscribers raving about their boxes enough to share? Take a look at what the people who have tagged images have said about the box. Which items have they particularly liked? Which boxes are getting the most shares? This will give you a great insight into what your similar ideal client is loving!

HOW DO THEY ADD VALUE FOR THEIR SUBSCRIBERS?

Are your competitors adding any extra value for their subscribers outside of just the items in the box? Do they have a community, learning opportunities or even money-off vouchers for things that they'll be interested in within the box? If they're not adding extra value, consider why they're not doing this. Is it because their subscribers just don't want any extra content outside of the box, or is it because they're not interested in extra value or is it because they're simply not being offered it? This is something that you can offer to your subscribers to help you stand out from your competitors.

ARE THEY RUNNING ANY SPECIAL OFFERS?

Later in this book we'll talk about how important it is to have an unmissable offer when you want to scale up your subscribers. Seeing what offers your competitors are running is super valuable as you'll be able to deduce what is working and what isn't by the social proof (comments) on their ads and social media posts. If they're not running any special sign-up offer, then it will probably mean that they're facing a bit of an uphill struggle to get people signed up to their box. If they are running offers, what kinds of offers are they and how would you value their offers? For example, if you're a dog box and one of your competitors is running an offer for a free dog bed, but another competitor is running an offer for a free dog camera, look at why someone may choose one over the other. What is more valuable to potential subscribers?

WHAT SOCIAL PROOF DO THEY HAVE?

What kind of social proof do your competitors have, both on their website and also on their social media? What are people saying about them outside of the context of a review? Really dig deep and see what people are commenting on their posts. What is the general consensus on the box from both the subscribers and people who are being served their content and could be potential subscribers for both your box and for your competitor's box.

HOW OFTEN DO YOU WANT TO SEND YOUR BOX?

There is no hard and fast rule as to the frequency of sending your subscription box. Boxes can go out monthly, quarterly, seasonally, bi-monthly or even weekly. The frequency in which you choose to send your boxes out is entirely down to you and down to your subscribers and the frequency that they'd like to receive them.

When deciding when to send out your box, it's key to think about the needs of your subscribers. Do they need something monthly, or would bi-monthly be better? For example, if it's a book box and you're sending a weighty tome each time, maybe a bi-monthly subscription will be best for your subscribers so that they can finish one book before being sent the next one.

Some boxes need to be more frequent, especially replenishment boxes. For example, if your box is focussing on sending out cat litter to subscribers, they won't want a quarterly delivery, as by then they'll have had to have gone out to the shop to buy more cat litter. This would render a subscription to automate the 'cat litter side' of owning a cat pointless. Always make sure that the needs of your ideal subscriber are at the forefront of your mind when deciding on the model for the box.

One of the key things to remember is that when you run a box that's quarterly or even bi-monthly, you're only going to be receiving payments from your subscribers four times or six times a year, meaning that your income will be half or a third of what it would be if you had a monthly subscription. The flipside of this is that you're going to have far fewer boxes to plan, far less fulfilment and dispatch paperwork. However, you will still have the same amount of marketing and customer service as if you were running a monthly box. Despite this, if a quarterly or bi-monthly box is what is right for your customers, fear not, you can still have a hugely successful and profitable subscription box business and you can easily upsell added extras and items to increase lifetime value when you've built your subscriber base of loyal fans of your box. Fab Fit Fun is an example of a hugely successful subscription box which ships seasonally and offers plenty of opportunity for upselling and cross selling.

When you survey your potential customers during your market research make sure that you ask how frequently they'd like to receive their deliveries and consider the answers carefully to ensure that when you launch your subscription box you've got the frequency and timings right for your new subscribers.

WHEN TO SEND YOUR SUBSCRIPTION BOX:

Deciding when to send your subscription box can be a challenging decision to make. The most important questions to ask when working out when to send your boxes are these:

- When do my subscribers want their boxes?
- Are they willing to wait for a box or are they going to want it straight away?

I run two different subscription boxes and they ship in different ways. With my box The Business Box we send the boxes once a month and everyone's box is shipped at the same time. There are many benefits to doing it this way, both from a subscriber point of view and from a business point of view. For our subscribers it means that everyone is expecting to receive their box at the same time. As such they're looking forward to its arrival as soon as the dispatch date comes. As The Business Box is a discovery box and all of the items we send are a surprise, it means that everyone receives their boxes at roughly the same time so when subscribers start to rave about their latest box on social media and in our members' community there's no opportunity for the surprise to be ruined.

Our Nutritional Ninjas Bake Box is aimed at children and as we all know, children don't like to wait for things that they're excited about. We send these boxes out as soon as the payment has cleared. If a parent signs their child up for a subscription on the third of June, the box will be packed and sent on the same day or the following day, depending on the time that it comes through. The same goes for their subscription renewals. We find (because it's a box for children that's primarily an activity) that often parents are ordering as they need something to entertain the kids – and fast, usually because it's the school holidays and it's decided to rain for days and Mum and Dad are tearing their hair out over how to stop the constant whines of, "I'm bored."

For these reasons, it suits our subscribers to have their boxes shortly after their payment has cleared. We run this monthly; therefore, if anyone orders or renews in the month of June, they will receive June's box. Once June has finished everyone will move on to July. The only time that this becomes challenging is when there are only thirty days in the month or during February when there are only twenty-eight. However, we have set our system to renew people's payments early if they originally signed up on the thirty-first of a month so that the payment comes out on the thirtieth, meaning that they always have a payment come out in each calendar month and therefore don't miss a box.

When your subscribers will want to receive their box isn't the only consideration you need to make when thinking about when you will be sending your box. The shipping cycle needs to fit into your own lifestyle and also into the way that you wish to work. In many ways, sending out the boxes all in one go is far simpler than daily sending. Firstly, if you're buying items from outside suppliers, it means that you can have all your items ordered and delivered ready for your shipping date. You're not having to have a constant supply of items coming in to meet the demand of new subscribers and payments renewing. You also have the advantage of the fact that each month's box has already been paid for by your subscribers long in advance of you sending them, helping not only with cash flow but also with knowing exactly what inventory you will need.

CHOOSING A CUT OFF AND SHIPPING DATE (IF SENDING ALL IN ONE BATCH):

Choosing when you cut off orders for each month's box and also when you ship is one of the biggest logistical challenges of starting a subscription box. The trickiest thing to get your head around in the first instance is when to open the cart on your pre-launch, when to cut off for the first batch of boxes and then when to ship the first boxes. The reason that this can be such a conundrum is because you want to ensure that when your new subscribers' payments have renewed for the first time that they have already received their first box, or it's on its way and arriving imminently. People will lose trust in your box and your brand if they have made two payments without receiving anything and it could result in people getting confused about your integrity as a new business.

When choosing a shipping date there are several things to take into consideration; I think that shipping around the middle of the month is best. That way, you're deep into the month so there's no confusion amongst subscribers about whether the latest box is (for example) February's or March's and also because the middle of the month gives people time to subscribe for the current month's box without signing up on, say, the third of June and then having to wait until July for their box because June's shipped on the first of the month. I'd also recommend avoiding dates around the twentieth to the twenty-seventh of the month, the reason being that when you hit December there are always delays with the postal services as they become more and more in demand. As such it's wise to avoid this time to steer clear of unnecessary delays at Christmastime when you'll naturally see a surge in new subscriptions and gift subscriptions.

The Workings

3

THE WORKINGS

PRICING:

When launching a subscription box, one of the most important things to get right from day one is your pricing. You want it to be profitable for you, affordable for your customers, and still maintain price integrity with your industry. Getting your pricing right from the start couldn't be more important. Having to put the price up for your existing subscribers at a later date will not only disillusion your subscribers, but it'll also look unprofessional on your part.

It's also important to mention that being the cheapest isn't always going to result in instant success. It might just mean that your ideal customer thinks you're too cheap and therefore is more inclined to go elsewhere as their perceived value is higher. In fact, it has been said that the best way to sell a £5000 product is to put it between a £7000 and a £2000 product. The reason is that there is a cognitive bias called anchoring, whereby we naturally choose the product with the medium price. If you think back to buying decisions you've made in the past, I bet you can think of a time you've chosen the middle price for something; it's a little like Goldilocks choosing which porridge to eat in *Goldilocks and the Three Bears*: the middle price isn't too high, and it isn't too low – it's considered 'just right'.

Given what you now know about anchoring, if your box is within an industry where there are competitors or similar boxes, and if you can make your box become the medium-priced box (between the cheapest and the most expensive) within your niche then you can take advantage of the psychological draw of the middle-priced product.

WHEN THINKING ABOUT YOUR PRICING THERE ARE SEVERAL THINGS YOU NEED TO CONSIDER:

The first is the cost of putting together a subscription box. The costs will differ hugely based on your box contents and niche. For example, a craft or ingredients-based box may have lower product / item costs but the labour costs of pre-portioning and measuring the items will be more. The items in a stationery box may cost more but the labour costs associated with packing them will not be as high, meaning that there is no real 'this is how much a box should cost' answer.

Other things to consider include your staff wages (don't forget to pay yourself), any tech costs, transaction fees (like

Stripe and PayPal fees), taxes, storage, website charges, box inserts as well as other unavoidable costs like postage.

Some costs will be recurring every month, like transaction fees, etc., so it is easier to decipher how much should go into your monthly membership fees, whereas others will be annual costs (like your website domain and hosting, email software) and should be split across the length of time you expect to keep that subscriber signed up.

COST PER ACQUISITION:

If you're planning to run any paid traffic, to use affiliates or special offers, then it's really important to know and to take into account your cost per acquisition. For example, if you are running Facebook ads and your cost per acquisition is £14 but your monthly membership fee is only £20 with a cost to you of £15 (and only a £5 profit margin) then that person is not going to be profitable until after their third month with you.

Knowing how long it's going to take for someone to become 'profitable' with you is key to making your subscription box profitable and should play a key part in your decision making when deciding whether to run offers, experiment with paid ads and when deciding on the length of your subscription terms.

GROWTH COSTS:

It's really important to not only plan for the immediate future but also to plan for the growth that you're hoping to achieve. It's imperative that you factor in how much you might have to pay someone to (for example) pack your subscription boxes each month or to manage your customer service once you get to the point where you will need help. It is good to have in mind the point at which you anticipate needing this help, whether that will be at fifty boxes, one hundred boxes or whatever number you estimate you will need the outsource. It won't be possible to do this on your own as you grow, so knowing that employing someone on an hourly wage or salary will cost XXX amount means that you can work out how many extra subscribers you'll need to pay for them across a year while still enabling you to be profitable.

CONSIDER YOUR PRICING STRATEGY:

One of the ladies in my free Facebook group 'So you want to start a subscription box?' asked why after launching her subscription box she had had all of her subscribers sign up for just a one-month box with no future payments due. In essence, it wasn't a subscription box, it was a gift box. When we deep dived into why this might have been, it was glaringly obvious that as she had set her one-off box price and her monthly recurring box price as the same, people were buying the one-off box as it posed less risk and didn't have any commitment.

We developed a strategy whereby she put the cost of the one-off box (or gift box) up by a large margin and set her monthly subscription box at the same price she had previously to encourage people to opt for the subscription as opposed to the one-off box. It worked and her subscriber numbers are growing month on month.

It's crucial to have a pricing strategy in place that encourages people to not only subscribe but to also stay signed up with you longer, to help them to see the benefit of a long-last subscription with you.

I always recommend rewarding commitment, whether that's for committing to a certain subscription length either paying monthly or by pre-paying in advance. I always recommend rewarding those people for committing with a lower monthly price. This also incentivises people to commit for longer.

DON'T JUST MAKE YOUR PRICING ATTRACTIVE WHEN SIGNING UP:

How many times have you signed up to something with a fantastic starting offer like your TV and Broadband package, which for the first eighteen months is a bargain £15 per month, but as soon as the eighteen months is over, it jumps up to £75 per month? We've all done it and it's a tactic which I think lacks integrity and encourages people to deal hop when a new deal comes up, as well as preying on those people who are less savvy at shopping around for new deals. This is not a technique I'd recommend for your subscription box.

If you've been launched for a while and having read this chapter, you're thinking that you now need to put your prices up, I'd I really recommend 'grandfather pricing'. This means that your original, early subscribers always remain on the same rates that they signed up with, meaning that they have access to their original rates. It's very difficult to tell your existing numbers that you're raising their fees as it will result in a huge drop off in subscribers and a vastly increased churn. It is far better to keep existing subscribers happy than to spend the money and energy involved in replacing them.

This doesn't mean that you can't offer cheaper rates to entice people in, but I'd recommend gently increasing your prices in line with your growth to enable you to drop down to the original prices if you feel like a special offer price is necessary, but never drop below what your original subscribers have paid. They'll feel short changed and at best may cancel and resubscribe under your newest offer, and at worst, will cancel entirely.

However, it shouldn't be overly necessary to reduce your prices as you become more established, have more social proof, recommendations, and better negotiating power. If you work on building a box that existing subscribers love and potential subscribers are desperate to get their hands on, then you'll never be short of people ready to recommend your box.

WHAT PROFIT MARGINS SHOULD I BE LOOKING TO MAKE?

I'm asked almost every day how much a box should cost, or how much profit margin people should be adding to their raw costs. Asking how much a box should cost is a bit of a 'how long is a piece of string' question, as the costs of items will vary hugely dependent on the type of items going in the box, the price point the customers are going to be willing to pay and also the individual set up costs will vary based on the different industries and specialisms.

I always advise my clients to aim for a 50% profit margin, therefore whatever the costs for each box are, your profit is 50% on top of that. However, I do always caveat that by saying that this may not be possible straight away. When you first launch your box, you will have fewer subscribers than you will do when you are more established. Therefore, when it comes to negotiating prices with wholesalers, you will have far more negotiating clout when ordering 150 items than you do when ordering fifteen. As your subscriber numbers increase, your systems and processes will be more sophisticated and therefore everything will become speedier, meaning that you'll be able to stretch your profit margins further.

HOW TO SOURCE PRODUCTS FOR YOUR SUBSCRIPTION BOX:

Sourcing products for your subscription box can be one of the hardest, but also one of the most enjoyable parts of being a subscription box entrepreneur. If your box is a discovery box it is important to ensure that you vary the type of items in each box but still maintain the same quality and number of items. If your box is a replenishment box, although the contents may remain largely the same each time, it is important to maintain the same quality box after box. Relationships with suppliers for replenishment boxes are more important because it is key that you build that long-term trust and that together you can grow your businesses.

YOU WILL NOT GET THE ITEMS FOR YOUR BOX FOR FREE!

One more time for the people at the back: you will not get the items for your box for free!

This is a key point that needs stressing time and time again. So many people assume that subscription boxes get all of the items in their boxes for free and that this is how to maintain a profitable business model. I can confidently say that this isn't the case. Although some of the bigger subscription boxes like Glossy Box may get some of the items for their boxes without charge due to the large following that they have and the awesome opportunity this gives their providers to get their cosmetics, skin care or make up items into the hands of thousands of their ideal clients, it is highly unlikely that you can expect your box items to be gifted until you've got many thousands of subscribers. You may occasionally get a few items offered as samples for your subscribers, but big, hero items will almost always have to be purchased.

YOU SHOULD ALWAYS BE BUYING AT WHOLESALE:

Now that we have established that you won't be getting the items for free, I'm going to tell you the secret of how you get great items for your box without paying full retail price, enabling you to not only get great quality items that would retail for far more but to also make a healthy profit on your box. This how you'll often pay, say, £20 for a subscription box and receive £60 worth of products. This is due to the wholesale price being far lower than the RRP.

Buying at wholesale means that you'll have access to bulk discounts for the items that you're buying. You can generally expect to save 50% plus on the RRP of items, although this does differ from supplier to supplier. In particular, beauty and cosmetics items often have very favourable wholesale pricing due to the large mark up on cosmetics. When you buy items at wholesale you will be subject to minimum order quantities (or MOQs as they are often called) meaning that you can only order a minimum amount. However, this is often relatively low, so buying at wholesale can still be achievable when you're starting out.

THIS IS YOUR PERMISSION TO GO SHOPPING!

One of the best ways to find items for your box is to hit the shops. Yes, really, this is your permission to go window shopping (or real shopping) to find all the items that you need for your box. One of the most successful ways I find items for The Business Box is by popping into lots of independent shops and seeing what they have to offer; I have a look around for the items which may suit my box and either buy them or take a photo of them, including a photo of the back so that I have the product number and the company it's made by. I then contact the company directly to enquire about wholesale pricing and order directly from them. The reason that I advise to start looking for items in small independent shops is because you'll normally find that these small independent shops will have already bought items from wholesalers with lower minimum order quantities, so in many respects they have built you a ready-made catalogue of wholesale suppliers.

WHOLESALE MARKETPLACES:

There are several ways to find wholesale retailers. Some will allow you to buy at wholesale straight away and others will ask you to create an account and submit some information like your company number or tax reference. The best way to start finding wholesale retailers is with a wholesale marketplace like Faire, Abound, Ankorstore or Creoate. All these feature a plethora of different wholesalers across lots of different categories for you to choose from. You can order directly on the website and your items are shipped from the individual wholesaler directly to you.

One thing to note is that the retailers on wholesale marketplaces will often be charged a percentage of your order by the marketplace and due to this they have often put their prices up to cover those costs. Therefore, once you have found a retailer you'd like to buy from on one of the marketplaces, it can sometimes pay off to contact them directly through their website to see if they have better pricing for buying directly. Not only does it potentially mean cheaper items, but it also means the supplier (who is often a small business) is not missing out.

SHIPPING FROM OVERSEAS:

Buying items on websites like AliBaba is a very popular way to obtain goods for your boxes. The plus side of this is that on the surface the items appear to be very cheap, sometimes just a couple of dollars for something which at retail would be three, four or even five times that amount. However, there are often hidden costs. Frequently, the shipping cost is more expensive than the actual item cost and you have to be wary of customs fees when they arrive with you. Also be mindful that shipping times vary greatly depending on the time of year you order them. (Chinese factories have an extended break for Chinese New Year.) They also vary based on whether they're being shipped by air or sea. Air is quicker but much more expensive and sea freight takes considerably longer, particularly if they are shipping on a shared container and need to wait until the entire container is full before it begins its journey.

Although the financial benefits are often still greater than buying direct from local suppliers, there are other pitfalls to consider. For example, you can't physically check the suppliers are making your products and that their staff are being treated ethically, nor can you chase up the progress of your order easily. Often the time difference and language barriers can cause stress and unless you have an agent working with you in the country where the factory is based and acting as the 'middleman', it can become tricky. Furthermore, from an ethical point of view, if choosing to buy from abroad please do make sure that the factory's working practices are in line with your own morals and brand values.

Two things to look out for if you are buying via AliBaba are the reviews on each seller's profile and whether they are verified by AliBaba. If they are verified then they have a certain level of kudos behind them which means they should be more trustworthy.

WHITE LABELLING:

One way to set your box apart from your competitors is to include exclusive items that can only be found in your box. You can use a product designer to design products from scratch and have them made to your unique specifications, or you can white label existing products. There are a limitless number of products that you can white label, from candles to cosmetics, skincare to sports items. The process involves selecting the items that you'd like to use for your box and then designing the labelling for those items. In some cases, you can personalise the items further, for example with specific scents for candles or specific ingredients in cosmetics.

White labelling is a great starting place for creating your own products. However, there may be high minimum order quantities, so it may be wise to wait until you are a little more established before pursuing this avenue.

MAKING YOUR OWN PRODUCTS:

Many people start a subscription box because they want to add a recurring revenue stream to their existing business and already make their own products. If you already make your own products, then you have a huge catalogue of your own items to choose from and the only limit is your own imagination. However, when your subscription box kicks off, you may find that your own time and resources simply aren't enough to keep up with demand, so it is key to have a plan in place to either outsource some of this work by teaching someone your skills and hiring them to make the items or to find another company that can cope with the demand. It's important to work this into your pricing so that when you reach your own capacity you don't 'shoot yourself in the foot' when it comes to maintaining your profit margins when you need to outsource some of the making.

TRADE SHOWS:

Trade shows are a fantastic way to see all the big suppliers in one place. Some trade shows will be industry specific whereas others will be more generic and focussed on a wide range of industries and will features a variety of suppliers. Attending trade shows is always a great use of your time as it not only allows you to put a face to a brand by meeting the people behind the scenes, but also gives you a chance to see the products up front and to check the quality without having to order samples. Occasionally trade shows will also have offers on for orders placed during the show – either money off or additional items for free.

NEGOTIATIONS ARE KEY:

When running a subscription box, we have an unusual edge over other suppliers in that we want large quantities of one item. When you start out and only need a handful of items, it's less likely that you'll be able to negotiate on the set whole-sale price. However, as you get more subscribers and you need more items and therefore you're putting more work (and money) the way of the suppliers, then you should be able to negotiate even on the wholesale price. The best way to do this is to first ask for the standard wholesale price, then ask again for a price on X number of items, and they may offer a small discount. If they're reluctant to offer a bigger discount, then it is worthwhile asking them what order quantity you'd have to reach to get your desired price. It's always worth trying to negotiate because even a 5% discount on a £1000 order is a significant amount saved, enabling you to increase your profits and offer better value to your subscribers.

IT'S ALL ABOUT THE OFFER:

When it comes to subscription boxes and particularly to growing your subscription box, 'the offer' is super important. There's a reason why the big guys like Hello Fresh, Gousto and Glossy Box always have a different offer running, because it's key to hooking new subscribers into their boxes.

Sometimes it can be scary as a new subscription box owner or as a box that's bootstrapped and steadily growing to break away from the mindset that running an offer is not going to be profitable. However, even if by running an offer the first box is a 'loss leader' (i.e. not making you any money) then all is not lost, as long as you have a robust strategy to reduce churn.

The first rule of running an offer for your subscription box is SUBSCRIPTION TERMS.

Let me say that again: do not run an offer without subscription terms.

We have all signed up to a subscription box, got the first box for free or half price and then decided to cancel the subscription as soon as the first box arrives or, in many cases, before it's even landed on the doormat. I've personally done it several times with Hello Fresh. I simply claim the free or half price box and cancel straight away. Why? Because I can; there is nothing in place to stop me from doing so.

I learned this lesson the hard way. When I launched my Nutritional Ninjas Bake Box during the lockdown of 2020, I knew that we needed an offer to hook people in. I didn't consider how we kept them hooked after getting their first box on an unmissable offer.

We offered the first box for free. It was a great offer and one which worked exceptionally well. I already had an audience built, so when it came to offering out the box to them, they jumped at the chance for a 'free first box'. We gained over one hundred subscribers in the first twenty-four hours of launching. Great, right? Yes, absolutely; however, we also found that within the first forty-eight hours of launching, our churn rate was at 50%. That's before even sending out the first box. I knew from this point that I'd made a major booboo by giving people the option to cancel at any time.

Don't make the same mistake that I did.

Having an unmissable offer is so important and having the first box for free is a great first offer to have and is always attractive to potential subscribers. But always, always ensure that you have subscription terms in place.

For example, we now offer the first box free with a six or a twelve-month minimum subscription and people are still happy to sign up and to commit. However, it means that we have far fewer of the 'take the first box and run' people. We have it set up so that people can claim their first box for free but even if they try to cancel, their monthly payments will continue until the minimum subscription term that they agreed upon when signing up is complete. If they had the first box free and committed to a minimum of six months of further boxes, they'll continue being charged until their minimum term is up.

Although it is tempting to think, 'Well, my box is fantastic. After they receive the first box, they won't want to cancel anyway,' no matter how fantastic your box is, how wonderful the concept is and the contents are, people will still take a first box free offer and run. Many won't even get to the point of receiving your fabulous box before cancelling. It's human nature to seek out a bargain and if you make it too easy for people to cancel after their first box then you won't be making a profit and your box won't be a business, it'll be an expensive hobby.

When it comes to subscription terms you can introduce them in one of two ways. I will talk about them in much more detail in the chapter on churn. You can ask people to commit and pay up front for their minimum subscription term (i.e. pay for six months as a one off payment) or you can set up your payment system (such as Subbly) to take the payment each month and not allow someone to cancel outside of their minimum term.

There are a number of different offers that you can run and there are advantages and disadvantages to all of them. Below I've broken down some of the offers that we have tested and how they've performed; which have proved most popular and which are ones we wouldn't run again.

One thing to note when it comes to offers is that they do fatigue fairly quickly. You don't want to run an offer for months and months on end. Firstly, your potential subscribers will know that the offer is always available and will delay signing up as there's no urgency, but also an offer may appeal to one potential subscriber but not to another.

DIFFERENT TYPES OF OFFER:

FIRST BOX FREE:

This is always a popular offer. However, you need to be certain that you can cover your costs and that you're not going to land your business in debt if it becomes super popular. With a first box free offer, subscription terms are more important than ever. Lots of people will run a first box free offer but sneakily charge a large delivery fee. Although the actual postage and packing fee is just £1.50, they charge £4.99 to cover the contents of the box too. It's obvious to any savvy subscribers what is being done, but as long as they're making a saving on the first box, they'll still feel like they're getting a good deal.

If you're considering a 'first box free' offer then I would recommend only doing so once you know your churn rate and the lifetime value of a customer. You need to be sure that in the long run you're only running an offer which will pay off and make that customer profitable. You need to know that by month two or three the customer will be a profitable customer for you. There is no point in running a first box free offer if the customers will only become profitable after six months; you need to be sure that they'll become profitable subscribers by their second or third payment and that their subscription term is long enough so that they cannot cancel shortly after becoming profitable.

FIRST BOX HALF PRICE:

There are two ways to do a 'first box half price offer'. The first is that they simply receive the normal monthly box that is due to ship to all subscribers (so if they sign up in February before your February cut off then they'll get February's box) *or* they receive a box straight away which is different to the monthly box which ships to existing subscribers.

There are pitfalls to sending the normal monthly box and advantages to sending a different box. Firstly, if you plan to offer the same box as your existing subscribers as the first (half price) box and someone signs up under that offer, they could have a long time to wait for that box. For example, if your monthly cut off is on the seventh of the month, but a new subscriber signs up on the eighth of the month, then they would have to wait an entire month to receive their box, which is not only frustrating to your subscriber but also hard to understand when as consumers we're so used to Amazon Prime next day deliveries. This could mean that you have some angry customers (by no fault of yours) simply because they find it difficult to understand why their box delivery will take so long.

On the flipside, if you ship a different box, but send it straight away, then this means that your new subscriber will get their box straight away, meaning that they don't have to wait any length of time before their box arrives and they're happily welcomed into the habit of receiving your box almost immediately. As consumers we've become really spoiled by the speed at which we can receive things these days, so when we are asked to wait for something it can be tricky to understand. One advantage of sending a different box out for the first box half price offer is that you can use up any leftover inventory. My advice when making up a different box is to ensure that you always send a 'like for like' box, so you include the exact same number of items in the box as your normal monthly box, so that the box your new subscribers receive is the same quality as they'll receive with your regular boxes.

One way to avoid new subscribers being disappointed when they sign up for a box and don't get the same box as other subscribers is to set the first full price payment to be charged shortly after their initial half price payment. Of course, it goes without saying that you need to make it clear that the next payment will be within X amount of time but by setting the next payment just seven or fourteen days later, it means that your subscribers will get two boxes in quick succession and fewer people will miss out on the excitement of their monthly box.

TRIAL BOX:

Offering a trial box, mini box or taster box is a good way to give subscribers a hint of what is to come in the main box. As above, I would only recommend doing this if you're offering it with subscription terms. However, having a cheaper starter box is a great way to introduce your subscribers to the box and to excite them with a taster of what is to come. One way that this starter box or trial box is particularly successful is if you are launching a box that needs specific items to enable your subscribers to really get the most out of the box. The trial or starter box is a great way for them to get their hands on the tools that they need to get started straight away when their first 'proper' box arrives. This would be particularly helpful for a craft box where you need specific tools to complete the craft, or even for a cake making box where the subscribers get the essentials that they'll need for lots of bakes going forward.

A trial box will tend to have fewer items in it than the main box or a half-price box, which allows you to keep your costs down. One thing to be sure of is that you explain that this is a starter, trial or smaller box that people are signing up for as the first box, so they're not disappointed to get a smaller quantity of items than they have seen in the 'proper' box.

Trial boxes should cost less than the main box and as with 50% off the box, I'd recommend having a swift turnaround for that second payment so that people can get the 'main' monthly box as soon as possible.

DOUBLE YOUR FIRST BOX FREE:

A double your first box free is fairly self-explanatory; the subscriber's first box contains not only the items from the normal monthly box but the same number of items again, free of charge. If you have a replenishment box, then these items can be the exact same as are included in that month's or quarter's box; if you have a discovery box, these items should be different but the same in number. For example, when we run this offer for The Business Box, we include two different books, double the amount of stationery and two items of self-care.

This is a great offer as people love to feel like they're getting something for nothing. However, as you're not discounting the price but doubling the value, you're attracting a different type of customer to those that are purely looking for a bargain as can be the case with reduced-priced boxes. This should create a better quality of customers and ensure that you're not attracting people who will churn quickly after they've saved some money.

When running a 'double your first box for free offer is that the weight and size of your box when it contains double the items may go up, so be wary of not landing yourself with a super expensive delivery charge. Also, be mindful that you'll need to make it clear that it's only the first box that has double items and that after that they'll receive the normal number of items; you can mitigate this by popping a note in the first box to explain that this is a super, bumper, double first box!

FREE HERO ITEM WITH THE FIRST BOX:

This has been one of The Business Box's best-performing offers. In November and December, we offered a free yearly planner by a well-known, well-respected brand for free for anyone who signed up for a minimum of three or six months. The planner was something that lots of our ideal subscribers were drawn to and many would have bought regardless, so getting it for free with their business box subscription was a great bonus and something which was a covetable item. The benefit of offering an extra hero item is that not only does it instantly give the subscriber a hint of what to expect from the box and the quality that you offer, but it also increases the overall perceived value of your box.

This is one offer that we will repeat over and over again with different items. However, we have found that it is key to have a great value hero product that people will want. There is no point in offering something basic like a notebook or a lipstick; it needs to be something which is of high value (potentially higher value than the overall cost of the box) to ensure that your potential subscribers see the benefit of subscribing and committing to get that item.

As always, be sure that you work out the cost of running this offer to ensure that it's not going to cost too much to run and will not make a subscriber unprofitable for a prolonged period. Make sure that you have worked out your costs and that you'll easily cover them with the subscription term commitment length.

How to Stand
Out From the Crowd

4

HOW TO STAND OUT FROM THE CROWD

HOW DO YOU STAND OUT FROM THE 'BIG GUYS'?

In many respects as subscription box owners, we can't compete with mega-corporations like Amazon. For a start, we're relying on outside delivery companies to deliver on time, so we can't get a box to our subscribers on the same day or the next day. Plus, when we start, we're often packing boxes at home on our kitchen tables and we have to rely on all the other cogs in the machine (like the items arriving on time, couriers turning up to collect boxes, post offices sending boxes once they've left you, etc.). In short, in these respects, we can't compete with the likes of Amazon.

However, a way we can compete is with the personalised service that we can offer. One way that you can do this right from day one of launching your box is to become the face of your box and your brand. This will help to grow that all-important know, like and trust factor ready to turn your subscribers into raving fans of your box.

Amazon, being a massive corporation, can't have that personal outreach and personal touch that we as smaller subscription box owners can. For example, if there is a problem with an order, we can reach out personally to our subscribers by picking up the phone or penning an email, without our subscribers feeling like they are speaking to a robot.

One way that you can stand out from the big corporations is by creating a community around your box. There are several ways that you can do this and by doing so, not only will you start to build that customer loyalty, but also your subscribers will be keen to share their great experience with their friends (who in turn may also be your ideal subscribers) and will hopefully encourage them to sign up too so that they can share the same great experience.

Here are a few ways that you can stand out and build a community around your box… which are *you* going to do to build that sense of community? None of these ideas will cost you a penny and all will help to build that customer loyalty, encourage your subscribers to share your box and reduce your churn. It really is a no-brainer!

START A SUBSCRIBERS-ONLY FACEBOOK GROUP:

As you've already learned from this book, niching your box down to target a specific type of customer is key. One thing that humans do is seek out people who have similar interests and similar experiences to us and by creating your own Facebook group for your subscribers, you'll be helping this process along. In an age when more and more of us work from home and can go days without seeing another human outside of our own four walls, it is more important than ever that we have the opportunity to connect with other people who are just like us.

Your Facebook group can be a place for your subscribers to ask for help, share experiences, discuss the items in the latest box and discover new tips and tricks to help with their shared pain points.

Running a Facebook group for your box doesn't need to take up lots of time. My recommendation is to set up an email to invite new subscribers to join the Facebook group after they've signed up and to sit down once a month to schedule content for your subscribers. Use things which will help to promote discussion and chats within the group. Once the group has become engaged and your members are all chatting to each other, then it'll near enough run itself as members will answer each others' questions.

SCHEDULED ZOOM CALLS FOR EVERYONE TO GET TOGETHER:

Human connection through the written word in a Facebook group is one thing, but being able to see people's faces and meet up for a chat online from the comfort of your home is a step above. Having a monthly meeting, coffee morning or Q and A can be invaluable for your subscribers. It will also help to position you as the expert in your field, helping to prove your knowledge on the pain points that your box solves and will again build up that all-important know, like and trust factor.

TRAINING OR ACTIVITIES ON A SPECIFIC BOX-RELATED TOPIC:

One of the key things that we offer with my box The Business Box is fortnightly business training by top business coaches. It helps our subscribers grow their businesses and adds exceptional value to our boxes. We host these on Zoom and they are recorded and added to our members' area for subscribers to watch back at any time. It also means that we have a bank of different training videos for our subscribers to access even before their first box arrives. It's become an invaluable asset to our subscribers and makes The Business Box more than just a 'box of stuff'.

Although we offer business training within The Business Box, that doesn't mean that you can't do something similar if your box is for a B2C client base. There are plenty of different training options that you can offer within your niche. For example, if you have a cookery box, you could offer live cook-along sessions or even pre-recorded videos for people to watch and learn new techniques.

If training isn't right for your box, then you could offer something like a monthly book group or a pub quiz night; the possibilities are endless.

INTRODUCE A HASHTAG FOR SUBSCRIBERS TO SHARE THEIR BOX:

A really simple way to not only build a sense of community but also encourage people to share your box is to have a hashtag for people to share on social media. The hashtag shouldn't just be the name of the box; it should in some way describe one of the advantages of the box. For example, our hashtag for The Business Box is #my favourite business expense which not only explains the type of box it is but also shows one of our key selling points – the fact that it's a tax-deductible expense.

The benefit of using a hashtag is that when existing subscribers or potential subscribers click that hashtag on social media, they'll see lots and lots of happy box customers, people who have been keen to go out of their way to share the box with others. It not only creates social proof but once again builds that crucial know, like and trust factor.

THE UNBOXING EXPERIENCE:

We've become so used to receiving plain brown, boring Amazon parcels filled with household essentials and other items, that we have become accustomed to ripping off the packaging, binning it and not thinking much more about it.

This is why a great unboxing experience as a subscription box can set you apart from your competitors and not only bring joy to your subscribers but also encourage them to share on social media, thus enhancing your reach and social proof.

THE BOX ITSELF:

The outer box/the actual box that everything will go in is very important. Often my clients doing my Tick all the Boxes course get worried that they've got to shell out for expensive printed boxes with high minimum order quantities from day one and this isn't the case at all. Although printed boxes are nice and they do help with brand identity, you can easily create a beautiful box using plain boxes and stickers and/or tape. One of my clients, Andrea, created Rebox, a mindfulness and self-care box and it's one of the classiest and most beautiful boxes. She uses a plain craft box and a custom eco-friendly water-based tape printed with her logo and some positive affirmations. The result is a beautiful, sustainable box which isn't printed or expensive.

People often ask about using plastic mailer bags over the top of their boxes to stop them from getting damaged in the post. I think that unless these are custom or in your brand colours they actually don't add anything to the unboxing experience and therefore are largely a waste of time, money and plastic.

The most important thing to think about when it comes to your box's arrival is how it's going to make your subscriber feel. Will they be overjoyed and excited to receive the box they've been waiting for before they've even opened it? Or will it be left in a pile with various other deliveries because it doesn't look enticing and exciting?

INTERIOR PACKAGING:

Keeping things safe within your box is important. You want to make sure that everything arrives in the way that you intended it to. Lining your box with tissue paper is a nice touch as it allows your subscribers to open the box a little like they're opening a present to themselves. However, when you get to the stage when you're packing hundreds or even thousands of boxes each month, folding and then lining boxes with tissue paper can become very tiresome and could add an extra day or two to the packing process.

Another way to keep things safe but still exciting is to use crinkle-cut paper. This is zig zag cut paper which is available in various colours and acts as a nice way of padding everything and stopping things from moving around.

If your box is food or something that needs to be refrigerated, then you'll need to look into a solution to get everything there so that it doesn't arrive melted or like mush.

PACKING LISTS AND PAPERWORK:

Packing lists serve a dual purpose. Not only do they tie everything in your box together nicely, but if the RRP of the items in your box is greater than the price your subscribers have paid for your box, then you have the added benefit of being able to display how much their box would normally have cost them if they'd bought all the items individually, thus emphasising the added value of your box.

Packing lists don't have to be fancy, they can even be on a label on the inside of your box, but what's key is that you're taking the opportunity to speak directly to your subscribers, check in with them and ensure that they're kept in the loop with what's coming up and that they're encouraged to share your box.

Some subscription boxes take it one step further and include a small magazine or workbook with every box. This can be a nice touch and something that you can build on as your box grows and develops, as running a small print run of magazines when you're first starting will be very costly.

In addition to packing lists, I always recommend including a 'hooray it's here' card which sits at the top of every box. It can be the same every month. It serves as a great prop for subscribers to use in photos. Make sure it includes all of your socials and your logo, so people know where their awesome box contents came from. It also helps to encourage your subscribers to share your box by prompting them with your hashtag and your social media handles to tag you.

BEING CHOOSY ABOUT WHAT GOES INSIDE:

It pays to be picky about what cross-marketing goes inside your box. As your subscriber numbers grow, companies that have the same ideal client as you may be interested in placing their marketing materials in your box. Although this will enhance your profit margins and enable you to make a little bit of money in advertising revenue, I always advise being very choosy about whom you feature in your box.

Make sure that their brand values align with yours and that there isn't too much of a crossover in their offering with what you're offering.

One of the most frustrating things as a consumer is when you open up a parcel and find 'half a tree' or multiple promotional bits of paperwork which don't get looked at and end up straight in the bin.

To avoid your subscribers feeling this frustration, always ask yourself whether the promotional material you're being offered is relevant, helpful and worthwhile including in your box. Always come back to your brand values and integrity and stay true to that regardless of how much money someone is offering to put their flyer in your box.

NOT MAKING A ROD FOR YOUR OWN BACK:

When you first start your box and you have lower numbers of subscribers, it can be tempting to 'go the extra mile with the packaging within your box, for example, wrapping each item in tissue paper or tying ribbon around the tissue paper in the top of the box. Although this will make for a fantastic unboxing experience, when you have hundreds or thousands of subscribers, this will be increasingly difficult to keep up and will mean that you'll need additional staff to help with this and will have to either pass this cost on to your customers or allow it to hit your profit margins.

It is very difficult to do something in the early days and then take this away and not offer it when you're more established, so always bear this in mind when starting to design your box and the additional packaging you're adding for your unboxing experience.

Pre-Launch &
Launch

5

PRE-LAUNCH AND LAUNCH

BUILDING AN AUDIENCE:

The most important stage of any business is building an audience. I'd go so far as to say that building an audience is *the* most crucial thing you can do to guarantee business success. That goes for any business, not just subscription boxes, but any business that wants to sell to their customers and scale.

Your audience is precious and even if they've not bought from you yet, it is important to nurture them and look after them by giving them lots of value even before they've spent a penny.

When starting to build your audience it is imperative that you know exactly who your ideal client is. Without knowing your ideal client inside out you risk attracting the wrong people into your audience and not being able to sell them anything further down the line, as they simply won't have an interest in what you do.

Growing an audience is more than just getting people to follow you on Instagram or to join your group on Facebook – it's about building a loyal following of raving fans. The overall aim of all audience growth should be to attract your audience to join your mailing list. The reason for this is simple. Social media posts are often either not seen or not engaged with. We scroll for miles on our phones each day and unless you have a particularly 'scroll stopping' post, it's unlikely that your audience, followers or ideal clients will stop by and be encouraged to sign up for your box. Furthermore, by getting someone on your mailing list, they have actively opted in to receive information from you. They're already a very warm lead and more primed to buy from you than someone who hasn't.

Although email marketing open rates can be difficult at times, if you can achieve a 20% open rate and have one thousand people on your mailing list, that's two hundred people actively opening and reading your emails. They're already warm leads and will be very keen to engage with your content.

Growing an audience doesn't happen overnight. It takes time and energy and can sometimes feel like an uphill battle or like wading through treacle. However, there comes a time when all of the things that you've been putting into place to attract the right ideal client into your audience clicks into place and your audience begins to grow.

There are many ways to grow your audience and the ways below are not the only ways to tackle audience growth. Some ways may work better for your audience than others and some may yield more results for different business types than others, so it is important to take a multi-layered approach to audience building.

When first starting to build your audience, I recommend putting aside a set amount of time each day to wholly focus on audience growth using some of the techniques below. That way you don't have an excuse to 'do it tomorrow – it'll become a part of your routine to be building your audience daily.

SURVEY:

In the research chapter, I talked about the importance of surveying your ideal clients and how this will not only be key to working out the needs and wants of your potential subscribers and provide relevant data for you to work from, but it'll also be the first step in building your audience. Not only will you be able to collect people's email addresses and share information about the progress of your box but you will also be able to gain crucial information on the places they hang out online for you to breadcrumb.

BREADCRUMBING:

Just like Hansel and Gretel left a trail of breadcrumbs to find their way home in the woods, breadcrumbing will leave a trail of information on how to find your box.

Breadcrumbing is all about going into the relevant online spaces and communities that your ideal client hangs out in and offering value, help and support to the members in there. You need to think of breadcrumbing as a way of helping people in an altruistic way. Although ultimately the aim is to get these people to come over into your audience, you should give as much value to them as possible to convince them to do so.

So how does breadcrumbing work? First (as with everything), you need to identify who your ideal client is and where they hang out. Imagine that your box is a children's cookery box which helps fussy eaters try more foods. Your ideal clients are mums of children who are fussy eaters. You know that they'll be hanging out in mummy Facebook groups. Your first port of call should be to search the group for any posts about fussy eating or anything related to that topic. If someone has posted about fussy eaters, now is not the time to go straight in for the sale; now is the time to offer value, offer advice and show yourself as the expert. It won't take long before other members of the group will be tagging you in relevant posts for you to give your advice.

At this stage, it is important that you have your personal Facebook page optimised and that it is clear you have a subscription box launching or already available to buy. People will naturally 'stalk' your profile to see what you're all about and they'll be able to see this clearly if you have your profile optimised.

Breadcrumbing is all about adding value, encouraging conversation and building relationships. However, don't expect to go into a group for a week and suddenly have a thriving audience. It will take time and energy to get the right people into your audience but when the ripple effect starts, it'll be worth it in the long run.

LEAD MAGNET:

A lead magnet is a free download of a PDF, video or something else of value that your audience can download in exchange for their email address. This can be anything at all that is valuable to your audience and relevant to your box. It could be a downloadable recipe pack, a step-by-step guide or a download of a meditation. The content of the lead magnet should be easily accessible and rapidly consumed as well as ultra-specific and relevant to your niche.

A lead magnet is a great tool to have in your arsenal when breadcrumbing. Not only does it allow you to become an expert in your field, to easily collect people's email addresses and instantly give you authority, but it's also something great to link to it in your personal Facebook profile so that people can see straight away that this is your specialism. This will supercharge your breadcrumbing as people will see this straight away when they land on your page.

A lead magnet must have high perceived value and be a worthy exchange for an email address. People can be precious over their email addresses and therefore only want to exchange them for something of real value and relevance to them.

It's important when building your lead magnet to have it set up so that everything is automated, your download is sent straight away, and the person who has downloaded it will receive emails which nurture them and further down the line introduce your box and what you do. Make sure that after these emails have finished, you're emailing the people who have downloaded your lead magnet regularly to ensure that they're kept warm even if they don't subscribe straight away.

COMPETITIONS:

Competitions are great for increasing brand awareness and social media followers, particularly as your subscription box will be very visual and will easily hook people into wanting it from photos alone.

The best way to run a competition or giveaway is to team up with a non-competitive business that has an audience of your ideal clients, but who doesn't necessarily offer anything which will conflict with what you do. For example, if your box was for new mums you could collaborate with a babies' clothing company to run a joint giveaway. You'll have a very similar audience but won't have any conflicts of interest.

Make sure that your giveaway prize is relevant to your audience and isn't generic in the sense that it's something someone who isn't your ideal client would want.

GAINING EMAILS FROM PEOPLE LANDING ON YOUR WEBSITE:

When you're in pre-launch and your cart isn't yet open, it's important that you have a way to collect people's email addresses. This can be in the form of a pop-up and using Wise Pops to co-ordinate this is effective as you can set the pop-up to appear when the customer is due to leave your website or has been scrolling for a few seconds rather than simply being a pop up that appears immediately and can be annoying to those who land on the website and want to scroll without being disturbed.

It is important to incentivise people to leave their email addresses in the pop-up box. This could be through offering them your lead magnet as I talked about above, or it could be that you offer them a discount to encourage them to subscribe.

We have had a great result with the spinning wheel pop-up feature. Not only does it gamify the process of entering your email address, but it also allows people to feel like they're getting a chance at a bigger discount and the temptation of this encourages them to enter their email. Furthermore, until they enter their email, they won't be able to spin the wheel and reveal their discount. The functionality of the wheel is great too, as you can set the different discounts you want to offer and how often it lands on them, so you could offer 10% off the first box to 50% of people, 30% off to 10% of people and so on.

CONTENT YOUR IDEAL CLIENT WANTS TO SEE:

Occasionally you might get lucky and some of the content you put out may go viral within your niche and you'll have a snowball effect of lots of new social media followers. However, the likelihood of this happening is not something you should rely upon.

Ensuring that you're putting content out there that your ideal client will resonate with is crucial. Not only will this enhance your chances of going viral and being shared by others, but it will speak directly to your ideal client and build that crucial know, like and trust factor.

All content should be relevant to your ideal client and should be either entertaining or educational. There is no point in putting content out there that is not relevant. When planning out your content, always think, 'Is this something my audience will resonate with?'

PRE-LAUNCH:

A pre-launch is best described as the warm-up before the marathon. It's the time when you're building your audience and building their excitement around what is to come. When starting a subscription box, having a strong pre-launch phase is key. Not only does it build the anticipation for the launch of your box, but it also means that the money from pre-sales can be used to buy the items for your first month's boxes, which is particularly important if you're planning to boot-strap your subscription box (launch without investment).

Your pre-launch process should be a minimum of six weeks of building excitement and anticipation, leaving oodles of your ideal subscribers begging you to sign them up. It's a period of building not only your audience of ideal subscribers but their awareness of what is to come.

Many people tell me that they want to start a subscription box but that they don't want to have to wait, or they want to skip the pre-launch. I'm afraid that unless you've already built an audience of the same ideal client that your box will appeal to and they're engaged and loyal, then skipping the pre-launch will likely result in your launch being a flop.

To give you an analogy, you wouldn't host a garage sale out of the blue, without telling anyone about it until the last minute, if you lived in a house in the middle of nowhere with no passing traffic or footfall.

In short, don't skip the pre-launch!

Previously we discussed your ideal client and how important it is to know them and know them inside out. However, during your pre-launch, this is when that ideal client work comes into play. Not only are you looking at who your ideal client is, but you also need to focus on *where* your ideal client is. Where do they hang out? Both in the real world and the online world. And how do you find them and make them aware of your box?

If you were looking to launch a box aimed at mums of pre-school children, then they'll be easy to find. They'll be at parks, children's classes, day nurseries and soft play areas. Or online they might be in Facebook groups aimed at parents of young children, or groups sharing tips on places to take under-fives in the local area, on forums and following mummy bloggers.

Knowing where your ideal client hangs out is key for your pre-launch. Throughout your pre-launch period, you're going to be showing up to your ideal clients, giving them lots of value and making sure that they know you as the expert in your field as much as possible. You'll be making sure that they know what's coming and ensuring that they know how to get their hands on your box when it comes to launching.

Your pre-launch is all about building your audience and getting 'eyes on the prize' or in this case, your box. The more people who see your box, the better. 'The rule of seven' was developed in the 1930s by movie producers who found that potential viewers needed to see a movie advert seven times before they committed to watching the film. The digital age with social media dominating means that as we're fed advertising and marketing at such an extreme rate it's now estimated that we need to see something two hundred plus times before committing to buy.

When I talk about building an audience, I don't mean building an audience of just anyone; you're building an audience of your ideal client who will hopefully want and need your box when it's available. You want to make sure that you're targeting all of your messaging toward your ideal client so that they know this is exactly for them. You could have an Instagram account with ten million followers, but if your subscription box is a box for dogs and their owners and your audience is made up of people who are allergic to dogs or don't like cute furry things then you're highly unlikely to be appealing to the right people!

Showing up and making sure that your ideal clients see you and your box time and time again during your pre-launch phase is so important and taking the time to follow the process laid out below will pay dividends.

STEP ONE: BUILD EXCITEMENT

Step one is all about building that audience of ideal clients. You need to think about where they hang out and the kind of content that they want to see. Get into the mind of your ideal client and think about the value you and your box can bring them.

A great way of doing this throughout your pre-launch (starting with week one) is to think about what subjects you can talk about as an expert which relate to your box. Your automatic reaction may well be, 'but I'm not an expert. You don't need to have a PHD or be a professor to be an expert in your field. After all, you could be the most rubbish wizard in the world but in a room full of mere muggles, you're the expert in wizardry. This is how you need to start to think about the subject matter of your box.

If you are launching a baking box for children, you could easily present a workshop for parents on tackling fussy eating, or on cooking with children in general. This will allow you to present yourself as an expert, and it'll be the perfect audience to get your box idea in front. If your box is for dogs you could launch a free PDF download on teaching a dog tricks and offer dog owners the opportunity to download it.

You then need to find places online or in real life where your ideal clients hang out. This could be in Facebook groups or physical settings 'in the real world. It's simplest to do this within Facebook groups but you could also use Instagram lives or do them in person too.

Once you've found a Facebook group which shares the audience that you're trying to target for your subscription box, contact the group admin (the owner of the group) to ask if they would be interested in you doing a free presentation, masterclass or workshop (or if you can share your free PDF) for the people in their group. 99% of the time they'll be delighted to have been asked and will be more than happy to have you.

If an informative presentation doesn't work for your audience or sit right with your box concept, then think about the type of workshop you could perform. It needs to be something which will add value and have people wanting to learn or see more (namely by subscribing to your box). For example, if you're putting together a yoga-themed box, you could do an online yoga session or a meditation to entice people to want to learn more about what you're doing. You want to aim to give enough value away for free that people know you as the expert, but it also leaves them wanting more.

When presenting a workshop or a masterclass, make sure that at the end you have somewhere to drive the participants towards. Ideally, that should be to subscribe to your box or to join your mailing list, but it could simply be to follow you on social media (or all three).

Building your audience takes time and is the most laborious process of launching a subscription box business. However, the bigger your audience and the more visible you are to your ideal clients, the better your launch is going to be. Audience building isn't just for your pre-launch; it's important to continue to grow your audience throughout your business journey. The larger your audience, the greater your success. This is why huge megastars like Kylie Jenner can make millions overnight by launching a new line of lip-glosses, simply because she's got a loyal and committed audience waiting to buy whatever it is she promotes next.

Being visible is key throughout your pre-launch and beyond. The marketing rule of seven suggests that a consumer must make seven interactions with your brand before committing to purchase; this could be seeing a social media post, watching a social media story, seeing a paid ad, or hearing about another subscriber's experience of your box or watching a masterclass.

As I mentioned before, this theory was established in the 1930s and although there is a lot of truth in it, the reality is that nowadays, with social media and smartphones making our exposure to information so much more saturated, it's more likely that you need to make ten or twenty times more than seven impressions to influence someone to subscribe to your box.

Having your box in the front of their mind by being visible and showing up every day will make your launch and the growth of your box even more successful. Make a conscious effort to show up every day, to do one thing each day to grow your audience. When I'm doing the small tasks to help grow my audience and wondering if it'll all be worth it in the end, I always remember how Ed Sheeran played hundreds of small pub gigs to tiny audiences of sometimes just three punters while couch surfing on friends' sofas until he became the megastar he is today. He put the graft in those early days to get the big break he needed to propel his career. In essence, he grew his audience and built a following and as the buzz around this young ginger singer-songwriter grew, word spread and he started to get noticed by more and more people.

STEP TWO: BECOME RELATABLE

In business, the phrase 'know, like and trust' is thrown around a lot and although building that know, like and trust factor is very important when launching your subscription box being relatable is just as important and will help to increase the number of people you attract and the number of people who trust you.

In the ideal client chapter, I talked about knowing your ideal customer's pain points and how your box solves them. This is where the knowledge and the work you put into establishing what these pain points are comes to fruition as it's going to form the basis of your content.

By being relatable, you'll pull on your ideal customer's heart-strings and they'll be able to empathise with what you're sharing, and they'll have a realisation about what your box will help them achieve or the problem that it will help to solve.

If you were launching a dog box, you could post about how hard it is to find healthy dog treats in mainstream supermarkets and how you have seen amazing benefits in your dog. If you're launching a craft box, you could talk about how frustrating it is to never have all the bits and pieces you need to complete a craft and how frustrating it is to have to source all the items. Or if you're launching a self-care box, you can talk about how you've suffered burnout after not practising self-care and how that affected you.

Becoming relatable doesn't have to be profound by any stretch. With my children's baking box, we speak to our ideal subscriber about how much parents want to bake with the children but how stressful it is to juggle the demands of work and family life. About how the mess can be out of control, with flour going everywhere, sticky fingers all over the kitchen and mum or dad ending up cleaning for hours afterwards.

Creating this relatability provides the perfect opportunity to explain how our box mitigates these problems, and how having the pre-packaged and pre-measured ingredients it means less mess and less stress. By highlighting a known pain point and expressing how our box makes this easier to manage, it works in such a way that potential customers can relate to the pain point and see that our box is the solution to that problem, swaying them towards subscribing.

As we are so often our own ideal clients, sometimes it can require becoming a little vulnerable when posting about these types of pain points and sharing personal stories. Think back to how these pain points have affected you; or, if you're not your ideal client, how they would make you feel and why it would be so important to you to find a solution to solve them.

Once you can become relatable to an audience of your ideal clients, then the know, like and trust factor can easily be built upon and by addressing your ideal subscriber's pain points directly you will help convert people into loyal subscribers who value how your box will help them to solve their problems and in turn will tell their friends who also share the same pain points.

STEP THREE: DANGLE THE CARROT... THIS IS WHAT'S COMING, THIS IS WHAT YOU CAN EXPECT, WHO WANTS IT?

Step three of your pre-launch is all about 'dangling the carrot. This is making sure that your audience you've been building is aware that something is coming. This is the time when you want to be sharing pictures of mocked-up boxes and showing them the type of items they'll receive and the quality that they can expect when they subscribe to your box.

A note on taking box photos:

The photos of your box are best thought of as your shop window for your subscription box. Make sure that you have good quality, well-lit photographs which are a great representation of your box. My advice is always to get a mixture of both flat-lay photos and photos of your products bulging out of the box. You need to make sure that your box looks packed with items that your ideal client will love and that they can see the value in them owning as well as knowing that it's been curated and created with them in mind.

When it comes to sharing photos of your box, I'd always recommend using mocked-up photos including similar items to those you'll be including in the box (making sure that they're of the same quality that subscribers can expect). Rather than using photos of your first month's box which will ultimately ruin the surprise, I'd share photos of sample boxes so that your subscribers get the true surprise 'happy post' experience when receiving their box for the first time.

At this stage, you want to be making sure that all eyes are on your box, that the excitement is building, and that people know the benefits of receiving your box at their door each month. One thing which will help to build the anticipation as you dangle the carrot is to share one 'hero' product from the first box. This could be a pair of sunglasses or a journal or, if your box is more about making something, it could be a close-up of the finished product without the need to reveal the whole thing.

This will give your potential subscribers the chance to see a sample of what they'll be getting. If they're excited about one of the products within your box and they know that there will be three or four more of a similar style and quality, then they'll be beating down your door to sign up when your cart opens.

STEP FOUR: HOST A VIRAL GIVEAWAY

During step four, it is super important that you keep showing up everywhere, sharing, promoting and pushing your box, making sure that you're turning up in all the places your ideal client hangs out, ready to make them aware that your box is coming.

As I've said throughout this chapter, the more eyes on your box during your pre-launch (and launch), the better it will be for the overall success of your launch and beyond. Sometimes we get lucky, and things go viral online, and they spread rapidly. However, other times it's not so easy and we need to give them a little helping hand.

Hosting a viral giveaway is one way to do this. You'll have seen time and time again on social media both small and large businesses doing a giveaway to try and get people to share, comment, like or tag their friends. This is a part of their mission to create more brand awareness and to build their audiences. This is the exact reason why using a viral giveaway in step four of your pre-launch phase is going to build your audience and help your launch fly.

There are several ways to help your giveaway go viral and to build traction, but make sure as you do so that the giveaway prize you're offering is relevant to your ideal client. Don't make it too generic like an Amazon gift card, which every man and his wife will want, but make it specific to your ideal subscriber. This will help you to attract the right people to your audience. For example, I wouldn't personally enter a competition to win a horse-riding saddle as I have no interest in horses or riding them. Giving away a short subscription to your box is ideal, or if you're not planning to launch for a while, perhaps a trial box or a selection of items similar to those you'd find in your box. In short, ensure that whatever your prize is, it's super relevant to your niche.

One way to help gain 'eyes on your prize' (quite literally) is to team up with other businesses that also have the same audience as your box. If you're creating a box for self-care for new mums, you could join up with a spa that offers mums treatments or a baby weaning brand to do a combined giveaway. That way you can both piggyback off the audience that you've both already built.

We can't guarantee that your box will go viral, or that your giveaway will, which is why using an app like King Sumo will help this along. King Sumo allows you to build your giveaway on their platform. You set the prize and it allows you to collect the email addresses of those who enter, enabling you to add them to your mailing list. However, this isn't all it does: after they've entered the competition, it allows them to gain additional entries by sharing to their social media platforms. For example, by sharing the competition to their Instagram story they might gain an extra entry to the competition; for sharing on their grid, they could gain two more entries; for sharing on Facebook they could gain two more entries, etc. That way, by the entrants sharing everywhere they possibly can, it'll help your giveaway reach to go further so that friends and followers of the original person entering can see the giveaway and they can enter too.

Make sure that you encourage people to enter their email addresses. Their email addresses are super important to your launch. (Of course, make sure that everything is GDPR compliant so that you don't run into any hot water.) Like, tag and share giveaways are great for increasing follower numbers but rarely transfer into sales as the number of people seeing your posts is likely to be very low. Only a very small percentage of people will see your social media content (it can be as low as 1-2%) whereas emails are usually opened and read by around 20% of people, hence having their emails and targeting them with a fantastic email marketing campaign full of value that's relevant to them and your box will be a much better way of getting the attention of your ideal customers and converting them into subscribers.

STEP FIVE: OPEN CART FOR PRE-ORDERS

This is, of course, the most important week as it's when you're asking people to part with their money. This is when the good work you've done in the previous four stages should start to pay off. Opening your cart should always be with a flourish. After all, it's what not only you but your potential subscribers have been waiting for. Make sure that before the cart even opens that your ideal customers know 'not to delay' and sign up immediately rather than waiting.

Having an opening offer is going to make signing up as a 'founding subscriber' even more attractive to people. This could be a special discount for a limited number of people (for example, the first ten subscribers get 50% off their first box) or anyone who signs up in the first twenty-four hours gets an additional item in their box.

Now that your cart is open it is even more imperative that you show up wherever your ideal client is, whether that's on your social media, as part of a Facebook group, or in someone else's network; you want to show up wherever your ideal clients are. Now is the time to share the box far and wide and make sure that everyone knows that this awesome box is out there, ready to solve problems and ready to delight your new subscribers.

Now is a good time to have influencers receive gifted boxes. It will give their audiences the chance to see exactly what's in your box; also, having influencers within your niche shout about how fantastic the items are is going to add to the overall excitement, will provide social proof and will also make sure that your box is seen by more people. Make sure that you check out the section on influencer marketing to learn how best to harness this new but incredibly powerful marketing technique.

STEP 6: CREATE FOMO

Creating FOMO or 'fear of missing out' is not just a jazzy acronym used by teenagers on Snapchat. It's a fantastic marketing technique that you can harness for your box once your cart is open and people have started to sign up. Often, when people are on the fence about something, seeing that the chance is slipping away and not wanting to miss out is going to be what gets them off of the fence and excitedly subscribed to your box.

There are several ways that you can create FOMO and in turn, create a sense of community for those that are already signed up. You could welcome each subscriber individually by sharing a welcome post on your social media which will help other subscribers be encouraged to become 'part of the gang' and will also help build further awareness for your box when your new subscribers share that post.

Another way to create FOMO and spread the message about your box is to create an image for your new subscribers to share on their social media to show that they've signed up for your box. It'll encourage their friends and followers to ask what the box is all about and could result in new subscribers who share the same pain points that your box solves.

By giving hints about what is in the box and showing hero products during your launch, it'll build not only the excitement but also the know, like and trust factor as people are excited to find out more and see what other goodies await them in their box. Time-lapse videos of boxes being packed and sharing how only a handful of boxes are left will help to get those that are 'thinking about it' over the line and ready to jump in head-first to subscribe.

Creating scarcity can also help to add to the FOMO for potential subscribers. If they know that there is only a limited number of boxes available or that your boxes could run out at any point, then they will be more encouraged to sign up quickly and to get off the fence.

A NOTE ON THE PRE-LAUNCH PERIOD:

There is no set time over which you should run your pre-launch. It could be six weeks; it could be six months. What is most important is that you are building an audience of your ideal subscriber. There is absolutely no point in rushing to launch before you're ready and before you've built up lots of 'eyes on your box'. It is important to remember that when building your audience, the numbers count. On average, only around 5% of people that are following you will see your social media posts, so even if you have one thousand people in your audience, that's only fifty out of one thousand people, which is why consistently showing up is so important. A post you put out on Monday may be seen by a different bunch of people than a post you put out on the following day.

Building an audience and going through the whole pre-launch process takes time and energy. However, if you put the effort in the early days then it will pay dividends in the long run when your box is out in the world.

LAUNCH:

Your launch should run seamlessly from your pre-launch. It is the time when your audience is most engaged, and you have been priming them for this very moment. Launching a subscription box is different to launching a course or a membership as it isn't an open and close cart launch. Once the cart is open, it stays open, and people can jump in and subscribe at any time.

Throughout your pre-launch, you'll have been building the excitement for this very moment, the time when people can order and get their hands on the box they've been hearing all about.

Building the excitement once you launch and with every new box cycle is key. Remember that people often won't see your posts and emails and will rely on your constant messaging to remind them to subscribe. It may also be that they've been following you and intending to subscribe but simply missed the notification that the cart was now open. I've lost count of the times I've launched something and done daily posts, daily emails, and personal outreach, only to find that after the cut-off date has passed someone emails me, disappointed that they've missed it! It just goes to show how important it is to be consistent and how easily things can get missed.

With the above in mind, please don't be disheartened if your launch doesn't see you have a sudden influx of subscribers. Often, if you don't have a huge influx in the first couple of days, it's time to reach out further and do some of the other things I'll be talking about in this chapter. Don't give up: your mindset will play a massive part in the success of your launch and if you start to lose faith, your potential subscribers will feel this too and won't subscribe.

Finally, before I talk about all the things you should do for a successful launch, please remember that before launching it is imperative that you grow your audience. Launching your subscription box to an audience of only a handful of people will sadly result in a disappointing launch. I'd recommend waiting and building your audience up further rather than launching too quickly. I've had so many people come into one of my courses or programmes having launched too quickly, lost faith and then lost impetus for their box.

There is no magic number of how large your audience should be. Instead, you should look at the engagement within that audience and how primed they are to buy; there is never a 'right' time to launch if your audience isn't big enough. Launching your subscription box is as much of a numbers game as dating is. Remember that even if you had a 10% conversion rate (which is very ambitious) from the audience to sign-up, if your audience is only one hundred people, that's only ten boxes sold.

CREATE FOMO:

Although this isn't an open and close launch, you can still create FOMO or 'fear of missing out'. This is because if you have a discovery box, your box contents will change month on month. To create FOMO you could share one hero product and explain how there's a limited supply, or have a special sign-up offer for those that sign up in the first month.

CELEBRATE THOSE WHO HAVE SIGNED UP:

You could also shout out subscribers who have already signed up; give them a graphic to share with their friends and family with the incentive of getting an extra item in their box if they share. By shouting out and congratulating those people who have signed up, you also get the opportunity to celebrate your new subscribers and make them feel welcomed into your box's family.

You could do this in any number of ways. It could be by placing their name on a pinboard of subscribers and sharing this on your social media, it could be by sharing a post about them, or simply by dropping them a message to say how excited you are to have them as a subscriber.

ENCOURAGE SUBSCRIBERS TO SHARE:

Your new subscribers are your best advocates. They'll know lots of other people just like them who are your ideal clients but who may not have yet seen your box. By encouraging and incentivising them to share, you can expose your box to a whole new audience.

One way to encourage people to share is to give them a discount or a referral code to share which means they essentially act as an affiliate for your box. The incentive could be a credit to spend on their future subscriptions or in your online shop, or the offer of extra goodies. Gousto does this very well. They offer all subscribers the opportunity to share their referral code and get £20 off their next box. The new subscriber also gets a free box, which makes it a no-brainer for them to subscribe.

SPECIAL OPENING OFFER:

Having a special launch offer can be enticing for people who have followed your journey for a while but equally for those who have just stumbled upon you. This should be a 'can't miss offer' to encourage people to jump right in and subscribe straight away. However, do ensure that your offer is going to not cost you more money in the long run and that you have subscription terms in place to ensure you don't have a mass exodus of subscribers after the first box. There is a lot more information on offers in the offers chapter.

LOGISTICS OF LAUNCHING:

When you've launched your box and you have subscribers signed up, it doesn't mean that the hard work is over. You need to make sure that you're managing your subscribers' expectations and that they continue to feel nurtured as subscribers in the same way that you nurtured them to sign up.

WHEN TO SHIP YOUR BOXES:

Deciding when to ship your boxes after your launch is a big decision. One trap you don't want to fall into is a situation where your subscribers will have their second payment taken before they receive their first box. You need to time this perfectly so that you have your first boxes shipped before anyone's payment renews. If your boxes aren't shipping immediately, make sure that you make this clear as lots of people will expect their box to land within days of ordering it and if they're not being dispatched until the following month, it is important to manage expectations.

EMAIL SEQUENCES:

Make sure that you have an email automation set up for anyone who subscribes to your box. This should be all about increasing the excitement and managing expectations about when they'll receive their box.

The email flow should be several emails long, with the emails spread out over several days or weeks until their first box ships.

The key things you need to cover in your email series are:

- Congratulating them on subscribing and when to expect your box
- Reminding them when to expect their box and keeping the excitement up
- Building a sense of community and encouraging them to share
- Revealing your hashtag and asking them to post on their social media about your box, featuring the hashtag and tagging you in (offer an incentive to do so)

A NOTE ON SALES:

SALES:

So many people are scared of sales. They'll say, 'I don't like selling,' or, 'I'm rubbish at selling,' but that doesn't have to be the case. Once you know who your ideal customer is and know how your box serves them, you know that you're helping your customers to solve a problem. It's important to flip your mindset so that you feel like you're helping them to access the best service (from you). You're doing them a favour by offering them your box and by selling to them you are helping them (not being an inconvenience).

Selling is not a dirty word. Selling is essential to the success of your recurring revenue stream and as we've established above, by selling your box you'll be helping people solve their pain points.

THE POWER OF POSITIVE LANGUAGE:

The most important and basic thing with sales is the power of positive language. Such a simple change can have a huge impact on your sales.

It's a habit we all slip into, but using negative language is one you must break when communicating with customers.

How often do you say at the end of an email, 'Don't hesitate to get in touch,' or, 'No problem,' or, 'No worries'? All these are big 'no-nos'. Simply change this to positive language to change the direction of the conversation. Words like *awesome, great, fantastic* and *looking forward to hearing from you* are all far better alternatives.

This simple technique is used by big corporations around the globe and there's no reason why you shouldn't do the same. Take Disneyland, for example. When asked, 'What time does the park shut?' staff (or cast members, as they're known) are trained to reply with, 'The park is **open** until 5.30 pm.' They focus on the positive. You can use this example in your subscription box very easily. If someone messages saying, 'I haven't received my box,' but they haven't shipped yet, you can reply with, 'We're so excited to dispatch your box on the eighth of the month.' Say this before explaining the intricacies of when the boxes ship.

WORK OUT YOUR CUSTOMERS' OBJECTIONS TO BUYING AND QUASH THEM:

Customers will always have objections to buying. These are often down to their own mindset issues. However, it is important that you manage these objections and address them in a way that flips their mindset into realising that your subscription or membership is for them.

For my children's bake box, we know that the main objections to buying are fairly simple.

DON'T BE AFRAID OF BEING 'TOO EXPENSIVE':

One common objection you'll get is that a product is too expensive. However, if Tiffany and Co can sell a paperclip for £190 then there is no such thing as too expensive... *if* you've worked out your ideal client. If someone says to you that what you're offering is expensive, it can be useful to explain the benefits and try to make your product seem like good value as opposed to expensive.

We quite often get people commenting on our Facebook ads to say that The Business Box at £35 is too expensive. We simply explain politely that although the subscription is £35 per month, the contents of the box alone are always worth more than £50, plus the added value of the business training is priceless. In truth, if someone is posting that something is too expensive, they're very likely not our ideal customer. However, that's not to say that the person commenting might come back in the future. By giving them an insight into the value, it keeps the door open for the future.

SETTING UP YOUR WEBSITE TO CONVERT:

Priming your website to convert couldn't be more important. You could have the most fantastic customer journey to get people to land on your website but if your website isn't primed to convert, they'll quickly bounce and you'll lose them. You could spend hundreds of thousands on Facebook ads and paid traffic, and run an incredible influencer campaign, but if your website isn't set up to convert to sales, or in this case subscribers, then no matter how many people land on your website, if your website isn't set up to convert they won't turn into subscribers.

If you study the websites of huge subscription box companies, there are several common themes. I have detailed all of these below and I'd recommend that you follow these tips rigorously. I have spent the best part of a year making tweaks and changes to our websites to enable them to convert better and have finally found the sweet spot by following what comes next.

REMOVE THE CLUTTER:

Having anything unnecessary on your website will kill your conversion rate. When it comes to your website, less is more. Lose any unnecessary text. People don't need to know your life story or why the business was started. Taskbars with lots of different pages can also prove to be a distraction that people can get lost on. I'd recommend removing these and focusing purely on the things that people need to see to convince them to subscribe.

CALLS TO ACTION:

You cannot have enough calls to action on your website. The main call to action that you need to push is *Subscribe Now* and this should be in every section. You should have this above the fold (the part of the website you see on your phone or laptop without scrolling down the page at all) and in every other individual section. Try putting it in a different colour so that it stands out from the rest of your branding and ensure that the process of subscribing is simple.

A PICTURE SAYS A THOUSAND WORDS:

With subscription boxes, a photo does tell a story. On your website, you need to ensure that you have photos of not just your box and its contents, but also photos of people with your box. For example, if your box is a children's baking box, you need to have photos of children completing your box, showing them enjoying the process and being super happy with the activity. The same applies to any type of box. Humans rely on connection and by seeing someone with the box to whom they can relate to, you can immediately build that know, like and trust factor.

STATE EXACTLY WHAT THE BOX IS:

When we launch a business, it becomes our baby and it's easy for us to assume that everyone else knows exactly what it is that we do. However, you need to consider how easy it is for someone who has never heard about your box before and has landed on your website to know exactly what it is that you do and who the box is for. For example, *A box of sensory goodies to help babies between the ages of three to twelve months with their development.*

Further down the page, you should also list out exactly what to expect such as *Two board books, one noisy toy, three messy play items and one treat for Mum and Dad.* You don't have to state the exact items, but giving a brief overview of the items that are always featured should pique the interest of your ideal clients and tempt them with of all the exciting things to expect from your box.

SOCIAL PROOF:

Social proof has never been so important. In a day and age when we can see many hundreds, if not thousands of adverts for different products and services a day, having that social proof in the form of testimonials, videos, screenshots, etc. makes a huge difference in convincing people to invest in your box. Using certified sites like Trustpilot or screenshots from reviews on your Facebook page or Instagram stories can make a huge difference to your conversion rate. It adds to that all-important know, like and trust factor and encourages people to take the leap of faith and sign up to your box.

MAKE IT EASY FOR PEOPLE TO PART WITH THEIR MONEY:

When someone has decided to sign up for your box, make it super easy for them to part with their money. Make sure that when they hit subscribe and start the checkout process, it is simple. If you don't need to ask questions like the name of their child or the name of their pet or their date of birth, then don't. All these seemingly small, inconsequential questions can cause a bottleneck in your process and mean people may abandon their cart.

Getting your website right won't happen overnight. It's something which will need tweaking time and time again to make it right for your audience. Websites can also get fatigued easily in the same way that offers can, so it'll pay off to update your website with new photos, offers and social proof frequently to stop people who are on the fence when it comes to buying your box from seeing the same thing, time and time again. Sometimes all it takes for someone who has been pondering your box for a while is a new photo that speaks to them and triggers them to finally commit to signing up.

INFLUENCER MARKETING:

Influencer marketing is a marketing strategy that has bull-dozed its way into the world of business since the rise of Instagram and YouTube. The rise of the influencer has taken place in as many niches as you could imagine; there are influencers in the cat world, cleaning influencers, horse riding influencers, and DIY influencers to name a few. Although it's a relatively new phenomenon. it's a phenomenon that's hard to ignore.

The personal brand has never been more important in our digital world and piggybacking off someone else's established personal brand is a powerful tool to help to grow your subscription box. In marketing terms, influencer marketing is a newer concept, but influencers are here to stay and their power can be huge – and if harnessed correctly can pay dividends many times over. It's well worth investing in a strong influencer campaign to increase brand awareness and build your audience as well as accelerate the know, like and (most importantly) trust factor, which is so important in business.

When I'm coaching subscription box start-ups, when I ask what their marketing plan is, they'll often put influencer marketing right at the top. And although they're right – it should be there – it's not a golden bullet. It needs to be used as part of a wider launch plan and not as something you rely on entirely to get subscribers. That's not to say you won't get lucky and have a huge influx of subscribers from an influencer within your niche who has shared your box, but influencer marketing should be used as just one cog in a wider marketing plan for your box.

WHO ARE INFLUENCERS?

Influencers can come under all sorts of different titles; some call themselves influencers, others call themselves content creators, and some would simply refer to themselves as celebrities. In short, an influencer is anyone who has built an audience within a specific niche. One influencer could be super famous in their niche and within their online world but in the real world would be passed on the street as just another normal 'muggle'. For example, take Mrs Hinch, the hugely popular cleaning and home influencer who shot to fame on Instagram and has millions of followers. Many people would 'fangirl' Mrs Hinch if they bumped into her in one of her favourite haunts, but many would walk straight past her, not knowing who she is or what she does. That's the beauty of being an influencer. They're famous within their world but outside of it, they could be anyone.

Since influencers are often famous within their niche but not necessarily outside of it, it is so, so important to get the right influencers for your box. For example, for my box, The Business Box, I wouldn't be looking to do an influencer campaign with Charli D'Amelio, the hugely popular TikTok star with tens of millions of followers. People who are looking to buy my box for female business owners or who are my ideal client are unlikely to be influenced by Charli despite her huge following.

When we talk about influencers, we don't just mean the big celebrity types with huge audiences of millions of followers or subscribers. Influencers with smaller audiences can carry just as much clout.

Influencers fall into four categories: mega influencers with more than a million followers, macro influencers with one hundred thousand to one million followers, micro-influencers with ten thousand to one hundred thousand followers and nano influencers with up to ten thousand followers.

There may also be other people within your niche who wouldn't ever dream of calling themselves an influencer. For example, in my niche, the business world for female business owners, the influencers that I sent boxes to when I launched were business coaches who had built audiences of their ideal clients who happened to be the same as mine. None of the people we sent boxes to would have classed themselves as influencers but had lots of influence over their loyal followings.

HOW DO INFLUENCERS WORK?

When thinking about influencer campaigns, it is key to remember that influencers, particularly micro and macro influencers, are businesses in their rights. They will take their content creation seriously and will be making and curating content that you can use time and time again. Many have invested in professional camera equipment, will edit photos and videos, and will wait for the right lighting to ensure that your box is shown in the best way possible. It's not just a case of taking a quick snap and uploading it.

The larger influencers will charge for their campaigns. Usually, the figure they charge will be based on the number of followers they have and the amount of engagement their account garners. This doesn't mean that there's no chance of one of the bigger influencers featuring your box on a gifted campaign basis, it just means that there's a limit to what they can do to maintain the engagement of their followers.

Gifted campaigns are the most popular when you're starting and trying to raise brand awareness. This is when you send the influencers a box for them to try. If they like it or want to post it, they'll share it with their audience. Be warned that they are under no obligation to post. They're also not under any obligation to say nice things about your box. They could state that they didn't like the box and wouldn't have bought it, or they could say that they love the box and will be subscribing. It's a risk you take.

One thing to note is that if influencers are doing their taxes and accounts in the manner that they should be, any gifted items are supposed to be classed as a taxable income, so if your box is £30, they would essentially have taken £30 in income, meaning that they then have to pay tax on that box.

FINDING THE INFLUENCERS:

Finding influencers is the easy part. The difficult part is finding the correct influencers for your subscription. For example, there's no point in asking a mummy influencer to collaborate with you when your subscription is for men who like fly fishing! The easiest way to find the influencers that your audience is going to be following is to ask your ideal clients and people in your audience whom they're following or what type of things they look for when it comes to the following someone online. When you find an influencer on Instagram that you think aligns with your audience and your brand, you can use the 'suggested for you' button which will bring up other accounts which are similar and whom the same audience is following.

Even if you have the most niche box in the entire world, I can guarantee that if you look hard enough there will be an influencer out there who will share the audience that you're trying to target. To start to find them, think about what hashtags they might be using. For example, if it's a box around balloon modelling (yes, this is a real box) you could look for hashtags like #myballoonmodel to try and find accounts that are posting the type of content which aligns with your box.

THINGS TO LOOK FOR:

The influencer's follower count is important but it's not as important as you might think. Followers can be bought, so if their follower count is suspiciously high and their engagement is low, then it may be that they've bought followers. It may also mean that even if their followers are genuine that they're not engaging with the influencer because they don't fall into the influencer's audience for the content that they're currently putting out. For example, if an influencer previously had an audience of young teenage girls and then has a baby and pivots into the mummy influencer market, she will essentially need to build her audience again as the original audience won't be as interested in the new content.

You can easily spot an influencer's engagement at a glance by comparing their follower numbers to the number of likes on their posts and views on their reels. It's easy to assume that an influencer with lots of followers will have great engagement but that's not always the case. Another way to easily spot if they've simply 'bought' followers is to look at the number of accounts that don't have any followers themselves or have bizarre names with lots of numbers behind them. If the majority of their followers look like this, then it would be wise to save your money and your boxes and look for another influencer within your niche.

You can check out an influencer's engagement on apps like Ninjalitics which will give you a percentage reading of that person's engagement when you enter their Instagram handle.

Sometimes engagement can be surprisingly low, especially for bigger accounts. This is purely because when an account has, for example, one million followers, the percentage of people seeing everything is still very high, even if their engagement is only 2%. 2% of one million people is still twenty thousand people. As a rule of thumb, micro and nano influencers tend to have better engagement because they tend to 'know' their followers a little better and their engagement is therefore higher.

The next thing to check is what they have posted before. Have they worked with brands? Have they worked with something similar to your subscription in the past, meaning that there may be a conflict of interest with what you offer? Also, look at whether they've posted any content that doesn't align with your brand values; lots of American influencers were dropped from brand partnerships during the 2020 presidential election for openly supporting Trump when his political views didn't align with that of the brand they were partnering with.

In the same way, if you're launching a subscription box of vegan snacks for animal lovers, it wouldn't be a good fit to go with an influencer who previously advertised an animal hunting expedition. Think about the influencer's 'brand image' and how that fits with your box and the values that you share. Make sure that they align, as a controversial partnership could do more harm than good.

HOW TO APPROACH INFLUENCERS:

In the same way that you wouldn't drop into a stranger's messages on Instagram and advertise your subscription to them (if this is a marketing technique you're using, stop now!) you need to first build a bit of a relationship with the influencers you'd like to work with. The best way to explain building a relationship with an influencer is to compare it to dating. You wouldn't walk up to a man in a bar and say, 'Want to have sex with me?' You'd probably end up with a restraining order. You'd start by introducing yourself, maybe having a drink together, having a dance and then seeing where it goes (a couple of nice meals out would be nice, right?) before jumping into bed. It's the same with an influencer. You want to 'wine and dine' them a little first. Become a name that they'll recognise before approaching them for a collaboration.

Don't be a stranger! On Instagram this is easy; simply comment and like their photos, watch their stories and comment using the reply box. Treat their page in the same way that you would treat a friend's, commenting and liking their posts. Make notes on what it is they're doing – if they've just moved into a new house, if they've started a new fitness regime, if they've been to a local restaurant, make a mental note of all of these things. After a couple of weeks of engaging with the influencer, it's ok to reach out to them.

When you message them or email them (email is best if you can find their email address), start by introducing yourself and before you launch into what you do, make sure to personalise the message to them.

For example *Hi Stacey, I'm Lauren. I've been following you for a while now and I loved seeing your adventures at Disneyworld last week. I took my son Joseph there last year and he's been begging me to go back ever since. Did you manage to try a Dole Whip at Magic Kingdom? They're life-changing!*

The first introductory part is the chit-chat that you'd have with a friend. It shows that you're a loyal follower, that you have consumed their content and that you'd like to get to know them better in the long run and work together. Once this part is out of the way, it's ok to then talk about your subscription box. Explain what you do and what you would like to offer them, whether it's a gifted item or whether you're looking to pay them for their content, and most crucially how it will help and appeal to them and their followers. At this stage, you don't need to explain the nitty-gritty of what you'd like them to do for you. You want to pique their interest. Once they're interested you can discuss the collaboration in more detail and what content you'd like to see in exchange for your gift.

Once they have replied, you can discuss what it is you'd like them to produce for you content-wise and the finer details. Make sure that you ask whether they're happy for you to repurpose their content onto your account, website or platform. Don't just assume that this is ok; make sure that they're happy for the content they've spent time on to be used. Generally, this is fine, but it's polite to ask.

WHAT'S THE DEAL?

It's important that you discuss with the influencer you're working with about what both of you expect from the collaboration. It is important to remember the value of what you're offering and to consider the amount of time it will take the influencer to create and share that content. If you run a subscription box which is £10 per month, then asking an influencer to post on all of their socials five times over two weeks with two grid posts, a story every day, and a reel of them using the box is not a fair exchange. For a box of this value, you're most likely to get a grid post and a story (from a nano influencer).

Although you don't want to lay down the law and demand too much, it's important to make it clear that this is a collaboration and you'd like to see photos and stories of the items you gift to them. It is also wise to ask whether they're happy for you to repurpose the images to use in ads or your own social media and to have this agreement in writing to avoid any difficulties in the future.

TEMPLATE FOR CONTACTING INFLUENCERS:

Hi (name),

I've been following you for (however long you've been following) and I loved seeing... (something they've been up to lately and have been posting about). I felt the same when... (insert personal experience that relates to you both).

I would love to share my (your subscription box) with you. I think you'll love it because... (the reason why they'll like it based on things they've posted before). I know that your account appeals to lots of... (whom they appeal to. Hint: It should be your ideal client) and I think they'd love to hear all about (your subscription) because... (insert reason it'll appear to their followers too).

If you'd like to receive a gifted (what it is you're offering) then please do let me know. Likewise, if you have any questions, I'd love to answer them.

(Your name and account you've been following them from.)

(Link to your website.)

MARKETING YOUR SUBSCRIPTION BOX:

The hard work doesn't stop after you've launched your subscription box. If anything, the marketing has only just begun. To keep growing and staying on top of your churn, you need to be marketing your box every day. There is no silver bullet when it comes to marketing your subscription box and although I list several ways you can market it below and although it seems daunting to have to consider them all at once, the beauty of running a subscription box company is that you can have systems and automations in place to help take the 'heavy lifting' out of some of this marketing.

EMAIL CAMPAIGNS:

Email marketing always yields fantastic results. This is because the people on your email list have actively opted to hear more about your subscription box, therefore: a) you already know that they're your ideal clients: and b) they're already warm (if not hot) leads.

You can set up several automations for your email marketing so that you're not having to constantly send out emails and you're not losing contacts when they join your list. I'd recommend as a bare minimum that you have a nurture sequence, an onboarding sequence and an abandoned cart sequence set up.

A nurture sequence is for anyone who joins your mailing list. This should be a series of around seven different emails which alternate between selling, adding value and building FOMO over a fourteen-day period. These should go out automatically so that when someone joins your mailing list they receive their first email (ideally featuring a special offer) within minutes and then are sent more emails intermittently over the two-week period to try and convert them into a box subscriber.

An onboarding sequence is another series of seven or so emails which are automatically sent out when someone subscribes to your box. These should build the excitement for their box's arrival but should also explain when to expect it, ensure that they know what to expect, and will also allow them to join any members groups, trainings, etc. that may be bonuses for being a subscriber. This email sequence is particularly important if you ship your boxes out on a specific day each month, to ensure that your new subscriber isn't expecting their box to ship immediately.

An abandoned cart series is really important. So often you'll be on a website, ready to check out, but get distracted or don't have the correct card to pay and therefore abandon your cart thinking that you'll come back to it later. It's the equivalent of putting everything in your trolley at the supermarket and leaving it at the checkout when you realise you've left your purse at home. Therefore, an abandoned cart sequence is an absolute must as these people are not just warm leads, they're positively hot leads. Your abandoned cart email should start straight away, as soon as they've left their cart. The first email should serve as a reminder that they still have your subscription in their basket as an, 'Oops, it looks like you left something behind.' After that, if they still haven't checked out, it is wise to follow up with an offer to entice them to visit the website and continue with their subscription checkout.

In addition to the three sequences above which run on automation you should be emailing your database at least once a week. These emails should not be purely sales emails. It is wise to alternate between sales emails and value-adding emails in which you share skills, entertaining content and tips that your ideal subscribers will want to hear about. For example, if you are running a cat box, you could send out an email about the top ten tips to keep your cat cool in hot weather, while weaving in that you are including a pet cooling mat in this month's box. You could send out funny stories about your cat to entertain your email database and encourage them to open your emails regularly including when it is a pure sales email.

Always remember that the people on your email database have chosen to be there; they do want to hear from you. So don't feel like you're going to be disturbing them with your emails. They are warm leads and you'll be doing yourself and your box a disservice by not following up on them.

CONTENT MARKETING:

In the modern world, content marketing is more important than ever. It's a truly valuable way of spreading the word about your box to your ideal customers without the need to spend any money. Content marketing is the images, videos and stories that you are putting out on social media to entertain, educate, sell to and inspire your audience. Content marketing is a fancy way of saying 'the stuff you put out on social media'. This can be in the form of videos, infographics, photos and stories. Content marketing does help to build that know, like and trust factor and helps people to see what goes into the journey of making your boxes.

There is no end to different content you could be creating and putting content out each day does sometimes feel like a full-time job in itself. However, I find that batching and then scheduling your content makes it far more manageable and better use of time than feeling stressed because you need to think about content on the fly each day.

Similarly to your emails, you want to use your content to: a) Show and share your knowledge; b) Entertain your audience; c) Sell your box.

Content marketing allows you to really show your personality (if you wish) and in turn show the personality of your box. The type of content that works well will differ drastically depending on the audience that you're aiming at. One type of content that works well for one box may not work well for another box. Packing and unboxing videos tend to do well across the board for subscription boxes. In the same way that children love watching other children opening Kinder eggs, adults seem to like the expected surprise of seeing what goes into each subscription box.

If you're ever at a loss when it comes to working out what content to put out, allowing your subscribers into the behind-the-scenes operations of the day-to-day running of your subscription box is always well received by both subscribers and potential subscribers. It allows people to go on the journey with you and again builds that know, like and trust factor with your audience of both existing and potential subscribers.

User-generated content is photos and videos which have been made by your subscribers. These look and feel organic as they've simply been shot on a phone in the moment. However, they serve a useful purpose in that they give potential subscribers an insight into the thoughts and feelings about your box direct from existing subscribers. This kind of content helps to increase the FOMO of people who aren't yet subscribed and the excitement of those that have subscribed.

PAID ADVERTISING:

Paid advertisements through Facebook, Instagram, TikTok, Google Ads and similar are hugely valuable and have their place. They allow you to get your box out there in front of an audience larger than you could ever dream of when doing so organically. However, I always, always recommend not running any paid advertising until you have tested your box out organically for a couple of months and you know that your numbers are all adding up and making financial sense. You also need to make sure that your website is converting and that your churn rate is low enough to ensure that you can afford the cost per acquisition you'll have for each sign-up.

Running ads through Facebook, Instagram and TikTok can be tricky to set up and can be very tricky to get right. If you're not technically minded, then it can be a lot to get your head around. Most importantly, you need a good understanding of exactly who your ideal client is to aid you in building audiences of the right people that your box is aimed at. However, once you know this, the results you can get from running paid ads can propel your box's growth like nothing else.

The beauty of Facebook and Instagram ads is that you're able to target exactly the people you want to be seeing your box. Gone are the days of running a television ad campaign and hoping that by playing it during a specific TV show that you'll get the right people viewing the advert and then going out of their way to visit your website to check it out. With Facebook and Instagram ads you can target the exact people you want to target. For example, if you want to target business-owning females between the ages of twenty-one and forty-five who are managers of a Facebook page, then you can do so. If you want to target mothers who live in London, with a child under a year old, and have an interest in baby-led weaning, then you can do that too. Even if you want to target male hairdressers who go to the gym regularly, you can do that too. It allows you to be as specific as you want to be with your targeting or as generic as you want, although as you've already identified your ideal client, you can save a lot of money in ad spend by only serving your ads to those people who are likely to buy.

As I mentioned before, paid social media adverts can be tricky to get right and a lot of testing needs to take place to enable you to find the sweet spot. For example, the content format that might work for some subscription boxes may not work as well for your box and vice versa. Running paid ads requires a certain level of technical knowledge as well as a certain level of patience and a keen eye for detail. You need to experiment with lots of different content, audiences, images, etc. to find the ones that work best for your ideal client. This testing phase alone can prove expensive, but don't skip it, as you need to find what works well for you. Once you find it and ramp up those ads you'll be 'cooking with gas' and your subscriber numbers will be increasing.

There is no knowing which ad content will work best for your box until you try it. The things that you think will be super popular are often not the ones which resonate with your potential subscribers. For example, we had some brilliant videos made for The Business Box and unfortunately, they didn't perform as well as we thought that they would as paid ads. To date, our best performing ad content is a photo of one of our boxes with four coloured pens laid on top of it. It's odd because it is the simplest of images and we have far more aesthetically pleasing photos which don't perform nearly as well. This is why the testing phase is so important.

Often, content which looks like it's been user-generated or which sits in the app and looks organic is a winner for paid ads. Twenty-first-century humans spend hours every day scrolling miles and miles of social media content for pleasure: we don't want to be disturbed by content which looks like an advert. We want to see things that look native in the app as if it's something that one of our friends has posted, helping to pull us from our 'scroll hole' but pique our interest enough to make us stop our scroll and visit the website to investigate further. Never has the need for 'native looking' ad content been more apt than with TikTok ads. TikTok's advertising advisors say that the best ads are those that look as if they're user generated. Their catchphrase is, 'Don't make ads, make TikToks,' to enable the ad content to sit stealthily within the app in the same way that all their other content does.

One other thing to note with paid social media ads is that they work best with an offer. As I mentioned above, we scroll miles of different content each day so to have your potential subscribers stop their scroll and take notice of your advert, it is advised to have a sign-up offer to entice them in. I talk about offers in the offer chapter, but it is worthwhile remembering that when running paid ads your offers can fatigue quickly and as such, you may need to change your offer every couple of months to entice people who haven't previously made the leap to subscribe.

PR:

PR is a great free marketing technique which will not only increase your brand's visibility but will also increase the kudos of your box too. There is no better way to increase your box's credibility than to be able to say, 'As seen in...' Working on PR can be a bit of a long game. It's not just a case of sending a journalist your box and them magically deciding to publish it in their glossy magazine (although that would be nice, wouldn't it?). It can be a case of pitching to multiple media outlets many, many times before you get a response.

There is several ways to get your boxes featured in the media. The first and most simple is to search for journalists and PR agents who are looking for specific items or stories within your niche. You can find these kinds of 'shoutouts' in multiple Facebook groups, but the easiest place to find journalists looking for specific items and stories is on Twitter where you can follow hashtags like *#journorequest* and *#PRrequest* and people will have posted about the stories that they're currently writing which need contributors. This could be for gift guides or expert comments.

It's useful when considering PR to think about the topics relating to your box which you can confidently talk about as an expert. For example, if you run a children's healthy cooking box you could become the go-to expert for fussy eating, nutritious meals for children, children's sugar intake, etc. You don't need to be hugely qualified, nor do you need to be the biggest expert out there to be the expert in your field. You merely need to be the expert in a room of 'muggles' to be able to provide comments in the press.

Having your own PR story will pay dividends. It will allow you to have an angle to pitch to the press. The story can be as profound as you want it to be, or it can be quite basic. It depends entirely on your background, your own 'why' your own story and how much you feel comfortable sharing. For example, with my children's baking box my story is about how I was such a fussy eater that I would only eat tinned mincemeat and frozen peas (yes, still frozen) until the age of six. At that point, I'd had multiple doctors try and intervene, and my mother had tried every trick in the book – that is, until she started to cook with me and found that if I had cooked something myself, I was more inclined to try the food and this is why I'm now running a children's cookery box. Having that story to hand means that I can speak from lived experience and contribute my story by pitching directly to journalists.

When it comes to PR, you once again need to know your ideal client and know what they read and watch. There's little point in pitching to Psychologies magazine about your dog box if your ideal subscriber won't be reading Psychologies magazine. Focus your time and energy on pitching to the media outlets that they will be looking at frequently to enable you to reach not only the right customers but the people who are actively looking for a box like yours.

INFLUENCER MARKETING:

We talked about influencer marketing earlier on in the book. However, it isn't a strategy to use just for launching. A strong ongoing influencer campaign can serve to give you a huge increase in brand awareness and the right placed influencer will bring new subscribers flooding in.

It is wise to remember that influencers need to be specific to your niche. There is no point in sending your box out to an influencer who has a big audience of people who are not your ideal client. When you're starting up, I would focus on smaller 'micro-influencers' with smaller yet still very engaged audiences who are likely to accept 'gifted' boxes as opposed to looking for payment as well as a gifted box.

You may not see immediate results from influencer campaigns. Sometimes it can be a bit of a 'slow burn'; however, running an influencer campaign has benefits in more ways than just driving sales. Influencers are often referred to as content creators and will be generating lots of content in the form of videos and photographs that you can use on your own social media channels. You'll also be growing brand awareness and building the know, like and trust factor for your box with not only your audience but the influencer's audience too.

Long-term relationships with influencers with the right audience can be super valuable and by gifting a box every time you shop, the influencer's audience will become familiar with your box over the months and will look forward to the regular unboxings. The frequency of the delivery will help to build an ongoing relationship between the influencer's followers and your box and will serve as a reminder each month of the existence of your box and hopefully prompt them to subscribe themselves.

One way to encourage your influencers to share and to get their followers to sign up is to give them an exclusive discount code for their subscribers. Not only will this help to convert their followers to subscribers, but it'll help you to track the results to see whether the influencer relationship is paying off when it comes to new sign-ups.

REFERRAL MARKETING:

There is no better marketing than word-of-mouth marketing and using your existing subscribers to recommend your box is a no-brainer. Not only are they already super fans of your work, but they're also advocates for what you do, and their friends, family and own social media audience will likely already be familiar with the box and therefore it'll already be on their radar. There are several ways in which you can set up your referral marketing scheme, but it is important to incentivise your subscribers to promote your box. This can be in several ways: it could be by offering them a discount off their next box, a free box for every person they have signed up with, or money back. If you have an online store alongside your subscription offering, you could also offer them credit or vouchers to spend within that online store. When deciding what to offer people, it is important to be generous, to incentivise people to share the box with their friends and encourage them to sign up. Offering something small will seem insignificant and people simply won't bother sharing with the same gusto that they will for something bigger and more tangible.

Setting up a referral scheme should be easy and all subscription-based platforms will have built-in referral tools which should be straightforward to get going. You will likely need to set up an individual link for each of your subscribers so that when used it can be affiliated back to them. With this in mind, when first starting it may be wise to set these up on a case-by-case basis when someone opts into the referral scheme. That way you not only save yourself some work but you start to build an army of super loyal supporters of your box.

To make your referral marketing a real success it is best to approach it with a proper strategy as opposed to just sending out a few links. I recommend putting together a pack of all the marketing materials which will help to sell your box. This should include graphics and imagery that can easily be used across your referrer's social media, swipe copy which can be copied and pasted into emails with sections easily highlighted for them to add their thoughts on the box, and information about the type of offers you're currently running and how they will translate for your referrers.

AFFILIATE MARKETING:

In some ways, affiliate marketing is like referral marketing. The difference is that it is companies promoting your box as opposed to individuals. There are benefits and disadvantages of doing affiliate marketing and this should be a marketing technique which is only used when you have a strong box that you know people love and you're on top of your churn rate / know how long in general people stay subscribed.

There are websites which are set up as specific affiliate channels. When you sign up to promote your box through them, people who land on their site will click through to check out on your website but in doing so, a cookie will be dropped which will allow the sale to be attributed to the affiliate channel.

Affiliate websites tend to have huge audiences so it's a great opportunity to get your box in front of large numbers of people. However, I would recommend thinking long and hard about whether it is the right audience for your box and whether the people looking at these websites are necessarily the type of ideal customer that you want to attract. When a website is called *freestuff.com* or *greatfreebies.com* it is likely to attract a certain type of visitor, namely those that are actively looking for a freebie that they can claim and then cancel straight away. As such, it is imperative that you are aware of this and enter an affiliate partner in the knowledge that many of the sign-ups will be people who will cancel straight away.

When working on affiliate channels it is imperative that you have a strong offer, normally a 'first box free' offer or a 'free mini box' offer. It is also very unlikely that the affiliate website will allow you to run any subscription terms, so you will be opening yourself up to a very high churn rate. However, there will be people who stay subscribed and who will love your box and be long-term subscribers. It is so important that you know the average lifetime value or life-span of a subscriber so that you know how long people stay subscribed and thus how long it will take to make a subscriber 'profitable' to you.

Affiliate channels make their money by charging you for each sign-up, in the same way, that you'll have a cost per acquisition for each person who signs up, regardless of whether they cancel immediately. I would recommend testing affiliate marketing channels after you've tested paid social media adverts as it'll give you a cost-per-acquisition price comparison between the two marketing mediums.

Although there are lots of pros and cons to affiliate marketing websites, one major plus point is the sheer number of eyes it will cast on your box. If people are going to be landing on your website from an affiliate channel, I would recommend having a 'squeeze page' which will mean that they can't progress forward to subscribe or claim their free box without entering their email address. As soon as they enter their email address, I would begin a nurture sequence which will hopefully convince them to sign up to your box in the future, whether or not they choose to do so immediately. This will not only be building your audience through your website but will give you a list of emails that you can use to both retarget and create lookalike audiences for Facebook and Instagram ads.

Maximising Your Profits

6

MAXIMISING YOUR PROFITS

CHURN:

Churn is a natural part of any membership or subscription. It's the term used to describe the number of people who unsubscribe from your box and is best recorded as a percentage of the overall number of subscribers you have.

Churn is a really important number to keep an eye on. If your churn is too high then you'll be constantly chasing your tail to grow bigger or to maintain the number of subscribers that you want. By industry standards, a churn of around 10% or lower is a good rate of churn. Anything higher than 10% and you will find that the growth of your box will be stunted, and you'll struggle to grow. Although 10% sounds like a very low number, if you think of it in the context of it being 10% of one thousand, that's losing one hundred subscribers a month and therefore having to gain another hundred subscribers just to break even on the previous month's numbers. You can see why keeping on top of your churn and having systems and processes in place is key.

I always teach my clients that when launching a subscription or membership, churn is a natural part of any business, but we need to do as much as we can to reduce churn.

Happy customers = Less churn (graphic)

Keeping your customers happy is imperative. The more you can keep them engaged with your brand the longer they will stay subscribed. James Sinclair of The Entrepreneurs University describes this as 'customer cuddles'. It's all about the extra special service that you can show to your customers to help keep them engaged and to transform them into raving fans. The more fans you have the more likely they are to recommend you to others, helping you to build a lifelong customer base.

Disney does this particularly well in their theme parks. Each year they hold an event at Christmas called Mickey's Very Merry Christmas Party. Guests pay an additional fee on top of their $100+ per day ticket to the park to see the Christmas parade and see Mickey in his Christmas gear. During the event (which isn't at all different to a normal day in Disneyworld) Disney gives out free hot chocolate and cookies to all the guests. Cute, you might think? How generous? This is Disney's way of making their customers feel special, to make them feel that they're getting something extra. We won't mention the extra $99 you've paid to attend the party or the fact that the cookie and hot chocolate only cost a couple of cents; when it's perceived as a gift from Mickey Mouse himself it feels all the more special.

The point is that Disney, a multi-million-dollar business, recognises the importance of looking after its customers and making them feel special. They recognise that sometimes the small things (like a free cookie) make their customers feel valued.

We should treat our subscribers in the same way. Make them feel valued and part of a family. If you can nail making them feel special, then you'll not only keep them as subscribers in the long run but will also have an army of loyal fans who will always promote your business at the drop of a hat. I recently experienced this when relaunching my theatre membership. I was relaunching post-pandemic after months of the theatres being closed. I asked my existing members to get behind me and support the launch, spread the word and provide testimonials or feedback to the people who were thinking about joining. With just one simple ask from me, they banded together and encouraged over five hundred new members to join my paid membership. There is no better marketing than word-of-mouth marketing, especially when it comes to a subscription box or membership, as it means that those contemplating signing up have the reassurance of real people who already enjoy your service.

TURN YOUR SUBSCRIPTION INTO NOT JUST A LUXURY BUT AN ESSENTIAL TOO:

Many people will sign up for a subscription or a membership to 'give it a go' and to see how they like it. Many will hop around different offers and bounce from subscription to subscription and unless what you do is very niche, you'll likely attract some of these subscribers too. It is almost human nature to not want to commit, to subscribe to something and cancel immediately if you have the option to do so.

Although we want the subscribers who are our ideal clients and who see the benefit of our membership straight away, we need to spend just as much time showing the subscribers who are 'just giving it a go' how valuable what you offer is.

With The Business Box, I have the physical subscription box element but also include monthly trainings. I noticed that what was missing amongst our members was that 'I've got your back' vibe, which as a solopreneur can be so valuable. In response to this, I added in a monthly 'hot seat Agony Aunt' call to which subscribers can bring their problems, issues and questions, and other members and I can add our thoughts to try and solve them. It's a really simple concept that only costs me an hour of my time but is invaluable for our subscribers and helps to make The Business Box not just a luxury but an essential.

Furthermore, by including the training as a digital element, the buzz of receiving the box is longer lasting and people are reminded about how fantastic their subscription is throughout the month, long after their box has been received and the items have been used.

HOW TO KEEP PEOPLE COMING BACK:

There are several ways to encourage people to keep up their monthly payments for your box and it's important to do a little bit of everything to keep your subscribers coming back and even begging for more. Keeping your existing customers happy is as important as new customer acquisition.

REWARDING LOYALTY:

Making a customer feel special because they've been a member of you for a certain amount of time is a fantastic way of keeping them engaged and signed up but also turning them into raving fans of your business. You want to be sure that they're telling their friends about you, mentioning you on social media and singing your box's praises.

One way you can do this is to reward people intermittently throughout the length of their subscription. For example, you could email them with a voucher code for money off their next box or your online shop (if you have one) when they have been signed up for six months. You could add an extra item to their subscription box for their third month's box or even just an email thanking them and offering a free trial for one of their friends.

One way that we have done this for The Business Box is to include a mini box inside the monthly box for the subscribers who have been with us for more than a year. We did so completely unannounced but popped a note into the box explaining that we are so grateful to them for being with us for such a long time that we've included a mini box for them to gift to one of their friends. This gives us a double whammy on the marketing front: firstly it's something to show appreciation for our long-running subscribers but it's also an opportunity to get our mini box into the hands of new potential subscribers who will hopefully be encouraged to sign up too.

The more you can make your subscribers feel special and valued, the more likely they are to remain subscribed long into the future. Something as simple as a handwritten note can go a long way, or a simple email that's personalised to them. For example, if someone has emailed to say that they're moving house and need to update their address, having an email scheduled for a fortnight to check in and see how the move went will be valued and makes the customer feel like you've gone the extra mile – without it costing you a penny. An example of this that I always remember is when one of the ladies within my theatre membership emailed to say that she wouldn't make a show that evening that she'd booked and paid for as she was having to have her dog put down. Being an animal lover, I simply dropped her a Facebook message to say that I was so sorry to hear her sad news and that I was thinking of her. Three years later, she's still a member and every year she messages me to say how touched she was by my kind message when the anniversary of her beloved dog's death comes around. Sometimes showing a human touch and proving that you are a business that really cares about their customers and not just about taking their money means that they will remain loyal to you for years to come.

It is important to look after your customers even when the going gets tough:

The importance of looking after your customers is never greater than when times are tough. Not only will this be a natural time for people to drop off but it's an exceptionally stressful time for you as a business owner meaning that you might naturally take your eye off the ball when it comes to looking for new subscribers. Treat your existing customers well and they'll be your biggest advocates for you and your box.

As I've mentioned before, in addition to running my subscription box businesses I also run a popular membership for theatre lovers. In March 2020 I had just relaunched my theatre membership and following the same process I write about in this book managed to welcome six hundred new members in less than twenty-four hours – three times my original stretch goal. Within a fortnight of this amazing launch, the theatres were ordered to close and the UK went into a lockdown lasting on and off for over a year. At the start of the theatre closures everyone, myself included, went into fight or flight mode as we tried to navigate through the tough times ahead. I came up with a plan to keep my members engaged even though they were unable to use the main benefit of their membership (access to cheap theatre tickets). In the first instance, we focussed on bringing the theatre to their living rooms, with exclusive live-streamed performances from West End stars. Also, knowing that everyone was missing connection, we included a fun quiz for our members, so that they could laugh along with it together.

As time went on and it was clear that lockdown wasn't going to be over as we had all hoped, we started to send out monthly gifts in the post to each of our members. These were hugely appreciated, especially when going to the shops for a little treat was off the cards.

These small things (as well as good communication and a strong history of looking after our members) all helped to enable us to keep the majority of our members during lock-down when their main membership benefit was impossible to use.

In times of economic struggle, or when we're being told time and time again by the media that times are going to get tough financially, like recently with the hike in energy prices, we naturally look to cancel things that we don't deem completely necessary. When news of the 2022 cost of living crisis was spiralling, Netflix reportedly lost two hundred thousand subscribers in the first quarter of the year. While Netflix had seemed like an essential during the lockdowns of 2020 and 2021, it was viewed as a luxury when people's freedoms returned. It is also estimated that a further two million people could cancel during the second quarter of 2022, the most in almost a decade. If Netflix, an enormous corporation with arguably the biggest clout in the TV and film streaming industry, are struggling with churn, it goes to show just how important it is to get a good grip on *your* churn from day one.

In times of struggle, emphasising the benefits and value of your subscription box is more important than ever. When the cost of living was due to rise, Netflix scaled back their benefits, disallowed password sharing, automatically upgraded everyone to an HD subscription, and cut back on new productions.

SUBSCRIPTION TERMS:

When you start, there is a temptation to introduce a 'cancel at any time' clause in your advertising. However, although this is tempting, it also leaves the door open to people who will just try something once and then cancel straight away. This is a particular trap if you're running a special offer as people will claim the offer and cancel straight away. I made this mistake when launching the Nutritional Ninjas Bake

Box. I spent time building my audience, went through the pre-launch and launched my box with an unmissable 'first box free', only pay postage and packing offer. People flooded to sign up to get their hands on a Bake Box for just £3.99. We had around one hundred people sign up within just hours of opening the cart. However, as the days went on, we saw more and more people unsubscribe. Why? Simply because they could. Some people unsubscribed before they'd even received the box, so we knew that the quality of the box wasn't the issue. The issue was that we had no subscription terms in place. If we'd had subscription terms in place, we'd have almost certainly had fewer initial sign-ups but the quality of the subscriber would have been greater and their lifetime value would have been far more.

It is beneficial to have some subscription terms in place to try and encourage people to stay with you for longer, especially if you're running an introductory offer. There are very few people who haven't subscribed to something for an unmissable offer and then cancel immediately because the option to cancel is there. If you remove this option then you are more likely to attract more of your ideal clients and fewer time wasters who are just looking for a bargain. It is human nature to fear commitment (and not just in relationships) so if someone is not your ideal client and is simply looking for a bargain they'll often churn straight away if given the chance.

We've already discussed the importance of having a great offer if you're doing evergreen selling (where your cart is always open) and adding in subscription terms will help reduce churn. It means that people who sign up for your unmissable offer will be tied into a contract of a certain length. Think of it in the same way as a phone contract. If you wanted the new iPhone but didn't want to pay £800 to buy it upfront, you'd take out a contract for a set amount of time so that you could walk out of the shop with the phone today but spread the cost over a commitment of X months. Having commitment terms in place is a very similar sentiment. Essentially your subscribers are committing to take advantage of your offer.

Subscription terms can be as long or as short as you need them to be to make them work for your business. Consider how long you need someone to stay subscribed to not only cover the cost of your offer but to also make them into profitable subscribers. You can set them to three months, six months or twelve months. Anything over months is unlikely to encourage people to subscribe as it will feel like too much of a commitment.

In Subbly (the system that I use for both of my boxes and highly recommend) you can set up subscription terms so that the payment is still taken monthly but that the customer is committed for a set length of time. Therefore, even if they cancel after one month, because they have committed to a certain length of time they'll be charged (and still receive boxes) until the final payment of their subscription term / their agreed contract has ended. Once the initial subscription term ends, I advise that you allow the payments to continue and the subscriber to receive their boxes unless they cancel. This means less admin for the customer and saves them having to re-subscribe.

You need to make the subscription terms super clear on your website and also in your terms and conditions so that this isn't a surprise to anyone if they are planning to take the offer and run. Your potential subscribers need to be well aware that they are committing to a minimum term when they sign up and that their payments will continue until that commitment term has ended even if cancelled early.

CONSIDER HOW YOU CAN GROW WITH YOUR CUSTOMERS:

Some memberships will see their customers naturally drop off when they outgrow the membership. For example, a membership for pregnant mothers will have a high drop off after six to nine months once the baby is born and pre-natal care is no longer a priority. It's important to have offers in place which mean that your subscribers can grow with you. If we take the example of the pregnancy box, it would be a natural transition to have a box which follows the transition to a new mum. It'll also increase your revenue stream and reduce your churn as you can naturally migrate people over to the next stage of their subscription as time goes on. Although it can be tempting to do something that is so niche that it 'times out' after a certain time (like the pregnancy box example), remember this will mean you're constantly going to be acquiring new customers to simply replace those who have churned, not because they don't love your box but because it doesn't accommodate their needs any more and there isn't an option available for them to continue their subscription.

CONSIDER YOUR PRICING STRATEGY:

When you're starting and considering how you're going to reduce churn, it's important to think about your pricing. Can you encourage people to sign up for longer or to pre-pay for a year or six months upfront to encourage them to stay with you longer? Not only will pre-paid or commitment terms subscriptions help forecasts (particularly if you're running a subscription box and need to know what inventory to order for future months) but it also means you'll have added cash flow to re-invest into your further growth like paid ads, marketing, PR, additional team members, etc.

MANAGE A PROBLEM BEFORE IT BECOMES A PROBLEM:

One thing that we can do to set ourselves apart is to have exceptional customer service, even when things go wrong. It's key to have fantastic customer service skills available to all but even more so when something doesn't go quite right. One way of finding out if there is a problem before it even becomes a problem is to send out a monthly feedback form a week or so after your boxes are dispatched. In the feedback form include three faces for subscribers to rate their overall experience of their box that month: one smiley face, one neutral face and one sad face.

For anyone who ticks the smiley face, send them back an email with somewhere to post a positive review of your box; for those commenting with a neutral face, reach out via email for more feedback; for the sad face, pick up the phone and try and see what they are unhappy about and whether you can make it better.

I have always been a believer that a phone call is always a better way of dealing with any issues than an email; things can get misconstrued when written down, but on the phone, you can always respond and react to the different tones in people's voices, something which is impossible to do over email. Furthermore, it's quite rare these days for things to be addressed via phone, meaning your excellent customer service will glow.

By being proactive and responding to anyone's problems immediately or before they even turn into problems, you can stay on top of your customer service and in turn stay on top of your churn too.

TRY AND SAVE CUSTOMERS WHO TRY TO CANCEL:

Trying to gain new subscribers takes lots of time and energy. If you're running paid ads to your box then it costs for every acquisition of a new customer, so it is more crucial than ever to try and save customers who want to cancel. One way that you can do this is to have a dunning sequence in place for when they try to cancel. As a bare basic, you should 100% include a question when someone cancels that asks them why they are cancelling; make this a multiple-choice question so that you can quantify the reasons people are cancelling and look to see whether there are any patterns in there. If there are, fix them before they cause you to lose more subscribers.

Having a dunning sequence in place will help to automate the process of saving subscribers. For example, when someone goes to unsubscribe from your box, they will be asked why they want to cancel; this could be for any number of reasons, but for The Business Box we offer the following reasons: too expensive, too frequent, too much stuff, environmental impact, not in business any more or other.

When a customer clicks one of these reasons, they'll then be redirected to a page to try and keep them as a subscriber based on the selection that they've made. For example, if someone clicks 'too much stuff' we offer them the opportunity to change their subscription to a quarterly box, still giving them access to our community and other benefits but ultimately meaning that they are only charged quarterly and only receive a box once every three months rather than monthly. If someone selects that the box is too expensive, then we offer them a percentage off of their next box. If they don't opt for this, we then offer them the quarterly box option. Give people options when it comes to cancelling to try and make it work for them and make the process of remaining a subscriber easy and accessible to them. It enables us to save them as a subscriber and keep them in our world for longer. Furthermore, nine times out of ten if a subscriber downgrades to a quarterly box, they'll see the hero product being offered in one of the boxes and ask to go back to monthly, which means that not only do we keep them as a subscriber, they'll return to their regular payment and shipment schedule.

Putting a dunning sequence in place takes a bit of time, but once it's in place it'll automate the process of saving subscribers for you and will in turn ensure that your churn remains low and your subscriber numbers remain high: it's a win-win!

PAYMENTS THAT BOUNCE:

Action Points:

- What can you add to your subscription or membership to make your subscribers feel valued?
- How can you make your membership or subscription a necessity and not just a luxury?
- How are you going to price your subscription or membership to encourage people to commit for a certain amount of time?

INCREASING LIFETIME VALUE:

When you've launched a successful subscription box you'll have a monthly recurring revenue coming into your bank account each billing cycle and that's great. There is nothing like making passive income and the reassurance of having a regular income stream will be a weight off your mind.

However, there is much more earning potential with your subscription box than just the recurring revenue from your monthly subscribers. As you've built your audience of loyal subscribers these people are already warm, if not hot leads to offer other goods and services. You already know that they are invested in your brand and know, like and trust what you do so offering them added value with additional things is a no-brainer.

There are several ways that you can increase lifetime value and therefore increase your profits and offer more value to your subscribers.

UPSELLING:

There are so many options for upselling within your box niche. An upsell is anything that you can offer as an extra. It could be a VIP box upgrade each month with extra items, premium delivery or an additional digital element. Or it could be a one-off box of related items. For example, if you run a craft box you could offer a box of tools and equipment to make their crafting easier or a complimentary craft for them to try out. Hello Fresh does upselling very well. They upsell throughout the checkout or menu choosing process. First, you're upsold to add additional meals into the box, whether that's to upgrade from two people to four or to add additional meals to take you from three days' worth of meals to four or five. Even as you choose your meals you're being upsold: you have offers to change the meats, to opt for steak or a premium meal. As you progress further, you're then offered dessert options as well as add-ons like bread, ready meals and even sandwiches. They know the value of offering additional items to their subscribers and how this increases their order value and thus increases their profits.

Although the above can all be done at checkout when your new subscribers are signing up for the first time (this is easily set up within Subbly) it is important to remember that you can upsell to existing subscribers; you don't just need to upsell at the original checkout point. You can upsell at any stage by contacting your subscribers via email or however you would normally contact them to let them know what you're offering. It could be an additional box, something extra like a hamper at Christmas, or a course in a complementary subject to the niche of your box. Using the audience that you've worked hard to build to offer them something which will bring them more value and more joy is not icky, it's good business sense.

Upselling is also a great way of using up any excess inventory. You can use your excess stock for things like mystery boxes and one-off boxes which will help with both storage and cash flow.

AFFILIATE SALES:

You've worked hard to build a committed, loyal audience and there will be other companies and small businesses that will be keen for you to promote their goods and services to your audience.

I always recommend exercising caution when working with affiliates. Your audience are precious to you and you don't want to offer them something that you don't truly believe in and haven't tried and tested yourself.

Every year I affiliate for my friend and mentor Lisa Johnson to help promote her course *One to Many*. The reason I do this is that I know how much the course impacted my business and how fantastic the course is. I'm happy to promote it and wholeheartedly recommend the course so sharing with my audience as an affiliate is a great way for me to add an extra revenue stream and also promote something I know my subscribers love.

DOWN-SELLING:

Down-selling can also be a way of increasing your lifetime value. I talk about down-selling a lot in the churn chapter. However, for those people who truly can't afford the subscription right now but would like to continue and stay in your audience, then down-selling them a digital subscription or a mini box is a great way to keep them engaged, keep them profitable but also to ensure that they remain loyal to the brand. They'll very often re-subscribe to your main offer when their finances level out again.

IN CONCLUSION

GET STARTED!

Starting and launching a subscription box doesn't have to be difficult. By following the steps in this book you can have a hugely successful subscription box business that brings you plenty of recurring revenue each month.

By starting your subscription box now, you're going to be in an enviable position as you can easily place yourself as the market leader in your field. Those waiting to start and enter the market in a few years will no doubt look up to you and your box as one to aspire to be like.

Use everything you've learned in this book to go forward and launch, scale and grow your subscription box to lofty heights and enjoy the journey along the way!

WORK WITH ME

I have had the absolute pleasure of helping many business owners and subscription box owners launch, grow and scale their subscription boxes. There is no greater joy for me than taking a seed of an idea and helping to turn it into a successful subscription box business.

To find out more about how to work with me, to ask any questions or simply to chat about all things subscription boxes, please email: hello@thebusinessbox.co.uk

To join my free Facebook group with lots of tips, tricks and advice on starting your box, simply visit: https://www.face book.com/groups/soyouwanttostartasubbox

Printed in Great Britain
by Amazon

19294103R00102